Preparing a Fruitful Harvest

One Mother's Pursuit of Generational Health

Autumn P. Prather

www.TrueVinePublishing.org

Preparing a Fruitful Harvest
By Autumn P. Prather

Published by True Vine Publishing Company
P.O. Box 22448
Nashville, TN 37202
www.TrueVinePublishing.org

Copyright © 2021 by Autumn P. Prather
ISBN: 978-1-7366672-0-0

All rights reserved. No part of this book may be reproduced in any form or by any electronic or mechanical means without permission in writing from the publisher, except by a reviewer who may quote brief passages in a review.

Printed in the United States of America—First Printing

To place orders for more books or to book the author for speaking engagements, visit: www.themotherdaughterexperience.com

Table of Contents

Dedication 5
Acknowledgments 6
Introduction 7
A Thanksgiving Surprise 11

Section 1: Preparing the Planter

Know Your Style 24
The ABCDs of Motherhood 36
The Viable Village 42
Self-Care 46
V.I.S.I.O.N. 55
Mama, You're Doing a Great Job 58

Section 2: Preparing the Soil

Love Languages 67
Your Tone Matters 74
Fear 78
Therapy is Necessary 83

Section 3: Preparing for the Seasons

Winter

Plot Twist 90
There is Purpose in Your Pain 96

Spring
The Fruits of Your Labor 102
The Fruitful Formula 108

Summer
Protect Your Fruit 118
Seek Your Passion 120
Fostering Friendships 126

Fall
Reap Your Fruitful Harvest 132
Leave a Lasting Legacy 136
Flip the Script 141

Dedication

To my late mother, Mrs. Linda Marie Page Everett and my late grandmother, Mrs. Rose Marie Hill Page. Thank you both for raising me to be a strong woman, to never be led by my fears but to always have faith. I am following in your footsteps, using your wisdom and the golden nuggets you left to raise my daughter, Sydnei Page Everett. That's the very definition of generational health!

Acknowledgments

To my wonderful daddy who is, literally, the best friend I never knew I needed and my phone buddy. Thank you for always being there for me. I love you so much. To my family—Frederick, Sydnei, Braxton and Braylon—you all are my rock and my reasons why. Thank you for motivating me to be my best self. I love each of you very much! To my friends and extended family who have helped me on this journey, thank you for your encouragement and support.

Introduction

First things first. My life is *not* perfect. My children are *not* perfect. My food choices are *not* perfect. My parenting style is *not* perfect. I'm *not* perfect. I have just been around for a little while and have learned a few things by trial and error. My family and I have the same exact issues as any other family—we fuss, we fight, we fall down, and we get back up. Mistakes are a part of life but giving and receiving respect (for ourselves and others) is always required.

Oprah Winfrey once said, "When you have more respect for yourself and put yourself in a position where you feel your sense of value or worth, that's how you know you're on the right path."

I believe, wholeheartedly, that the concept of self-respect and self-worth should be introduced very early in a child's life—especially a daughter. Before I became a mom, I always told myself that I would do things very differently than my mother. She did not talk to me about puberty and sex. I had to learn it all on my own, through reading the encyclopedia, watching TV, and talking to uninformed friends. When I started my menstruation cycle, I was totally blindsided. I was 11. I had just come from my first concert starring New Edition. My mom literally handed me a sanitary napkin and said, "Here, put this on."

I didn't know what it was or how to put it on. She also gave me a calendar and tried to explain how to count the days.

"So, I am going to bleed for a whole week? Am I going to die?!" I was so scared.

I remember this like it was yesterday. I also remember how I felt—totally lost and confused—and vowed that if I ever had a daughter, I would make sure she was well aware of her body, what it does and what it is capable of doing. As soon as my daughter turned three years old, I taught her the real names of her body parts. You know, "boobs" are called breasts. It is a vagina and not anything that starts with a "p"—things of that nature.

I wanted her to learn the actual names so that she could begin to respect the importance of her body and its functionality and to know that it is to be protected and revered. I also started talking to her about puberty as young as nine years old because I knew that girls could start their cycles around that age. I graphically explained what would happen when she began her period and how she would have to care for herself during this time.

We talked about what it meant to have a cycle. Simply put, it means that you are now capable of having a baby. It means you have to be very vigilant with keeping yourself clean and safe. More in-depth conversations would evolve over time as she got closer to tween age. A big topic was "stranger danger," even with familiar friends and family, and what to do if someone tried to touch her in unacceptable ways. We also set up a family password that only we

Preparing a Fruitful Harvest

knew. If anyone walked up to her and said that she was supposed to come with them, she would ask them for the password. No password, not going with you!

Beginning as young as three years old, I have told her that she must respect herself first or no one will; to lead by example; to not follow the crowd but to create her own lane of influence and impact; to surround herself with other like-minded people so that she can consistently grow and be the best version of herself at every level; and to work her vision plan, always being aware that life requires us all to pivot and/or to start again.

I drove the point home that by respecting herself and her body, she could keep herself as safe as possible. I taught her that by having boundaries and protecting her space, she sends a clear message that she is not the one to mess with. It also reiterates a oneness with and belief in self. What she feels about herself ultimately plays out in all areas of her life. Call it home training or whatever you'd like, but she was going to be set up on a path of seeing the true value of knowing her worth. No discounts allowed!

Motherhood is one of my best and most joyous accomplishments! I wanted to really do a good job with this new and challenging task as a single mother. That was 21 years ago, and a lot has happened in that time. I've been married and divorced, lost the two most important women in my life—my grandmother and my mother—and experienced many setbacks. I have also had many successes and proud moments. Writing this book is one of them. Along this journey, I have come to realize that raising a daughter is one of the hardest jobs in the world, especially in a world that is insistent on making some women and girls feel marginalized or disenfranchised.

I believe that women and mothers are a girl's first role model, and it is our duty to plant seeds of love, understanding, and wisdom to reap a fruitful harvest of leaders, trailblazers, trendsetters, role models and future mothers. We can break any of the strongholds and interrupt the patterns that do not serve us.

It is my hope that you glean something from my story of raising my daughter and find little golden nuggets of what you can do as a mother or a mother-figure in helping our young girls to navigate this life by planting the seeds, tilling the soil, and embracing all seasons.

A Thanksgiving Surprise

November 1998

I had just celebrated working my first year in the "real world" in corporate America, putting my business administration degree from THE Tennessee State University to good use. I chose to live with my grandparents after graduation because it was a peaceful place for me. But, they had rules! One in particular was to be home before midnight. Now, how in the world is this possible when the party's just getting started at 11:00 PM? I was feeling the itch to be on my own and being a young 22-year-old, I wanted a bit of freedom. *Shoot! Who am I kidding?* I had a boyfriend, so yes, I wanted a lot of freedom. So, I called up a realtor friend of mine and inquired about the home buying process.

"Well, Autumn. First I'll need to get you in touch with my preferred lender to run your credit and get you pre-qualified." she said.

My grandparents had bought me a car a couple of years prior, and put me on the loan as co-owner so that I could build up my credit. I wasn't worried about that part at all! Even though I was young, I was determined to start my young, adult life checking off all financial boxes–gainfully employed, good credit, and a homeowner. The realtor and I looked all around the areas of where my job was located as I thought this would be best because my normal commute was about a half hour drive. I was looking forward to less traffic and being in a new environment, basking in the feeling that I was moving out of town. I had lived in Nashville, Tennessee all of my life and was ready to move to the next level in my young life, even if it was only 30 minutes away.

Townhomes were big in the late 90's, so I was focused on getting one of those. It would be just enough for me... and, eh, my boyfriend (shhhhhh don't tell the parentals!). It was a pretty fast process as the housing market was booming back then. The realtor and I looked at about five different townhomes and we settled on the one on Strand Fleet Drive. What caught my eye was the beautiful acrylic ivy painting that lined the walls of the living area. Ivies were a special sign for me! Also, it was just so cute and quaint. I was getting excited about the next big move.

"WOW! I am about to be a homeowner!" I squealed to myself. No one knew this secret but me.

My closing date was set for September 30, 1998. Because I was a year into my career and lived with my grandparents, I had saved a good amount of money already. So, my down payment was locked and loaded! I felt so grown!! Now, all I had left to do was tell my parents and grandparents what I had done.

My grandmother was cooking in the kitchen, so I sat down at the kitchen table. My mom was at the house as well, sitting in the den area.

"Hey Ma. Come in here!" I said excitedly.

"Yes?" she said as she entered the kitchen.

Preparing a Fruitful Harvest

"Ma, I bought a house!" I just blurted it out.

My grandmother turned around with the spatula in her hand and said, "Really? Is that what you want?"

"Yes ma'am." I said, respectfully.

"Okay then." My grandma was a sweet, soft-spoken lady.

I went into detail about the process. "So, yeah, Ms. Jean helped me to find a house. You remember her from church, the realtor? It's a townhouse on a zero-lot line in Antioch. It's $70,000 and my down payment is only $3,500. I am getting an FHA loan. My closing date is September 30th." I was trying to sound all professional and like I had done my homework. We were about a month away from closing.

"Well, that's nice," my mom said in a carefree way, after the initial shock wore off. She was a one-liner kind of mom. She never gave long, drawn out responses. She cut right to the chase and always gave it to me straight, no chaser.

To this end, I was surprised my mother was as supportive as she was. I honestly thought she would chew my head off and give me grief about it. My dad, however, was not pleased. I guess he still wanted me to be his little girl. He had many questions about security systems and safety, as he should have. I tried to answer his questions with the confidence of an impending homeowner.

My mother and I quickly got to work picking out my furnishings. We went to lots of consignment shops and junk stores to find discounted gems. I wanted to decorate in all white and so we bought a white couch and loveseat, a white dinette set and an all-white bedroom set. Again, I felt really chic and grown!

October 1st came, and I was all moved in. My dad made sure the alarm system worked and all doors were secured. After my parents did one final check on the house, the outside perimeter, and the shed in the back, they left me there, all alone. I immediately started feeling anxious.

What have I done? I am all the way out here in no man's land, living on my own. I have to cook all my own meals and wash my own clothes now, I thought to myself.

Yes, I was spoiled living with my grandparents. I really didn't have to lift a finger. But that was part of the attraction and incentive to go out on my own. I wanted to learn who I was as a person and experience true independence for the very first time. I was grown in age, but not necessarily in experience, and I wanted to change that.

For the first few nights in my new home, I slept downstairs on a pallet in the middle of the living room floor. I wasn't ready to migrate up the stairs to my white bedroom in this oversized townhouse. I wanted to be close to the exit door so if I needed to escape quickly, I could. I think I was letting my dad's fears about security get the best of me.

Later on that month, I began planning my housewarming party. All of my close friends and family were invited to come and see my new place. *My* very own place! I was overly concerned with stowing away my boyfriend's things in a closet so no one would know that he lived there too. But somehow, someone got a little more curious and opened the one closet door I thought no one would open to see the evidence that I was not the only occupant of that quaint two-bedroom townhome. When my guest looked at me with a judgmental smirk, I just smiled and reminded myself that I. Am. Grown.

Right?

***

Thanksgiving is my all-time favorite holiday. Thanksgiving weekend 1998 would turn out to be a complete surprise that would change the trajectory of my life forever. When I woke up on Saturday morning, I didn't feel all that great. Something just felt off. Then, I checked my calendar. My cycle was 10 days late. I decided to take a pregnancy test.

As I pulled out that white stick, I asked myself, "Oh my God! What if I *am* pregnant?"

My heart began beating so fast, I thought it would come out of my chest. After I soaked the strip (TMI?), I placed the pink cap on it and laid it on the side of the bathtub. The two-minute wait time felt like two years. The instructions stated that if I saw one pink line, I was not pregnant. If I saw two pink lines, it was a positive result even if one of the pink lines was faded. My two minutes were up. I actually waited an additional minute to make sure I gave the test time to really finish. I hesitantly turned my head to the right, looked down at the side of the bathtub and gazed at the two pink lines.

Panic struck me like a lightning bolt. I re-read the box. *Who knows, maybe I misread the instructions.*

"NO!! NO!! NO!!" I shouted.

This was not in the plan. How could this happen? Surely I was smarter than this. I had bought a house. I had chartered a graduate chapter of Alpha Kappa Alpha Sorority, Inc. I had checked off several boxes of what it meant to be a responsible young adult. A baby? I had just decorated my new townhome with all white furnishings. I just spent a good chunk of my savings on this new house. This house was supposed to be my new baby, not a *real* baby. I am sure I was in shock for about an hour just sitting there in the bathroom staring into space. I made a call to my boyfriend who didn't take the news all that well. Turns out he was already expecting a child with another woman, so he had to go!

What a mess! I was pregnant and threw the father of my child out of my house.

Welp! I thought to myself. *I am keeping it, so I guess I need to get busy trying to figure out how to tell everybody else.*

First up were my parents. Then I was going to tell my grandparents the news that their little girl, who had made them so proud with all of her accolades and accomplishments so far in life was now about to be an unwed mother. See, I had already worked out my life's plan. I would graduate from college, work in my chosen career for about

Preparing a Fruitful Harvest

two years, get married, have my first baby at age 25, purchase two dogs–a Labrador Retriever and a Poodle, have my second baby at age 27, have my third baby at age 30, and retire at age 55 and travel the world in an RV for the rest of my life. Nevertheless, reality set in that my plans were being overshadowed by real life. I was about to be a mommy in nine months!

In my new house I had a long staircase. I sat at the top of the stairs, staring down to the foyer, with the phone in my hand. Since I had already made up my mind that I was planning to be a mommy, I needed to let everyone—*who needed to know*—know this new development. I kept playing different scenarios in my mind. Would my dad yell at me? Would he give me the silent treatment? Would he allow me back into his home? These are the negative things that ran across my mind and prolonged the inevitable phone call I needed to make.

It took me hours to muster up the courage to dial those seven digits. I was in pure agony—sweating, nauseous, heart palpitating and on the brink of a stroke or heart attack. I checked the clock, and it was around 6:00 PM, so I knew my dad would be home. I started dialing the home number and when he answered after two rings, I went silent. I was paralyzed with fear.

"Hello. Hello," he said.

"Hey Wema," I said.

I never called my dad "Daddy." I actually called him by his first name but in the only version I could say when I began to talk. His name is Waymond, but I couldn't say

17

that, so I said "Wema." Wema means Daddy in my language.

"What's wrong?" he questioned. He could hear the fear in my voice.

After a deep gulp, I let it rip.

"I'm going to be a mama."

"Aw. Is that all?" Those four words were like an elephant lifting up off of my chest. A burst of the coolest breeze came across my face. My heart slowed. My stomach settled.

"YES!" I was totally relieved.

"When?" he asked excitedly.

"I don't know yet. I'll be going to the doctor next week to find out."

I had the biggest smile on my face.

WHEW!!!

My dad was, unexpectedly, not phased about me becoming an unwed mother. In fact, he was so excited about the new addition to the family, he immediately asked if I knew what I was having. "No, I am only about eight weeks," I said, as I laughed through tears of joy that I had not let my dad down.

Now it was time to tell my mother.

"Hey Ma!" I said much more calmly. Besides, I had already defeated what I thought would be the "Goliath."

"I am going to be a mommy."

SILENCE. For about 10 seconds.

Then she spoke. "Well, my worst nightmare came true."

Preparing a Fruitful Harvest

I was heartbroken. "Nightmare?" But my dad was so happy! How could this be a nightmare?

I decided to give her a moment. More like a week. She finally came around and accepted it.

"Well, I guess we are having a baby," she said matter-of-factly. That was more than enough for me.

During the first few weeks of my pregnancy, I became engrossed in researching everything about my body and the developing fetus. I wanted to know what was happening in there, what I should and should not expect and what I needed to do to have a successful journey. I remember being giddy while purchasing the book *What To Expect When You're Expecting*. It was all scary and exciting. Whenever I had my doctor appointments, I would research the different terminology used and try to learn all I could about the various tests, such as Alpha Fetoprotein, amniocentesis, CVS, and ultrasounds.

In March of 1999, I learned I was having a girl. I wanted to know what could happen to her in utero. I wanted to know the statistics of chromosomal abnormalities. I wanted to know my options, pre- and post-delivery. I was making it my mission to bring my baby girl into the world as healthy as possible and I wanted to be as prepared. This was particularly important to me because I wanted to be smart about this new detour in my life. I did not want to be a statistic.

If you can't tell by now, I grew up surrounded by strong women, namely my late grandmother and my late mother. I was the beneficiary of their uncompromising family values and traditions, their prayers, unconditional love, undying support, and determination. So, I have always used my ma and grandma as a blueprint for how I would, one day, raise my daughter. My goal was to make sure that I was instilling all of those little golden nuggets of faith and family into her, as they were instilled in me.

I had a pretty uneventful pregnancy with no sickness. I only gained 22 pounds. My hair and nails grew like a weed. I moved back in with my grandparents during the last two weeks of my pregnancy because I needed to be close to family and the hospital. I felt wonderful throughout the whole experience. I normally have high blood pressure and take medication, but for nine months, my blood pressure was superb, and no meds were needed. I loved pregnancy but vowed to not become a single mom for a second time.

I went into labor at 5:00 AM on July 30, 1999. Because I had done so much research, I noticed one of the classic signs of labor. I ran to grab my labor manual and read the chapter that talked about the mucus plug. "Oh boy! This is it," I thought. Instead of getting prepared to go to the hospital, I wanted to take a shower. Hey! I wanted to be clean. But, before I got in the shower, I called my mom to tell her that I was in labor. I hopped in the shower and before I was done, my mom was there, at my grandma's house, ready to take me to the hospital. Talk about a speed racer!

We packed the car and started on our way to Baptist Hospital for what would become the first and best day of the rest of my life. I labored forever and at 4:45 PM, I was told to start pushing. I slept in-between pushes. It was exhausting, but at 7:30 PM, I was finally dilated to 10 centimeters. I gave a few big pushes and at 7:46 PM, I became a mother of a beautiful, 7-pound, 14-ounce baby girl named Sydnei Page. Page was my mother's maiden name. It is also my middle name. Sydnei is named after my great-grandfather, Sidney Page, my grandfather's father. Her name is definitely generational and intentional. It serves to remind her that she is from good stock. It served to remind me that I have the awesome responsibility to raise her up to be better than me and to go further than me.

Section 1

Preparing the Planter

Planter: A person who establishes ideas or principles. Additionally, in agricultural terms, a planter is someone who cultivates the land and grows crops on it. This book explores how the planter (mothers, mother-figures, or mentors) can produce a fruitful harvest in their daughters, young girls, or mentees.

In order to be a successful mother, you must first be an empowered woman. As the planter, your ploughing begins when you get clear on your style of parenting; learn the ABCD's of motherhood; realize the validity of the viable village; know the importance of self-care; and create your V.I.S.I.O.N.

Know Your Style

"Yes, I am a hovering 'helicopter mom'!" I told my close-knit friends who are all mothers. "I own it and I claim it."

The group went silent. Then, one of the mothers finally spoke up.

"But sis, you're going to ruin her. She's never going to be independent if you keep smothering her. Chill out and let her live."

My girlfriends would often debate me about what age was "grown" and what age was "legal." They would tell me that she was indeed "grown" at 18 and didn't have to ask for my permission or tell me anything regarding her life if she didn't want to. I begged to differ. I told them that as long as I am financially responsible for her, I get to call the shots. And for me, that meant at least until she finished her undergraduate studies at Tennessee State University. I don't care about a number. Besides, we are not living in the same world we were raised in during the 70's and 80's.

But still, I thought, "Hmmm...Could they be right?" I mean, I was very overprotective, sometimes obsessively. I had to be involved in everything. It was the only way I was assured she was safe and sound.

It was February 2018, and Sydnei was a second-semester freshman in college.

Preparing a Fruitful Harvest

"We are going to Panama City Beach for Spring Break," she said in passing.

"Excuse me? Who is going to Panama City Beach for Spring Break?" I said with an attitude.

All I could see in that moment was Natalee Holloway, the young, American spring breaker who vanished in Aruba 12 years prior and made international headlines.

"Also, you don't *tell* me anything. You ask," I continued.

"Okay so can we go? It's five of us," she said, still not really giving me any insight into this impending catastrophe that was playing out in my mind.

"No ma'am. It's six of us going." I sharply stated. "If you go, I have to go as well. I am not comfortable with releasing you to the wild like that just yet. I don't care if you are 18. You were just in high school last year."

"But ma—?"

I interrupted, "It's a no for you if it's a no for me."

"UGH! Okay. Fine!"

We started planning for the eight-hour road trip scheduled for March 1st, getting our attire together and mapping out the quickest route. It was decided that we would leave at 5:00 AM, so that we could get to *our* spring break beach vacation before sundown. I was so excited. I had been talking about taking a vacation for quite some time, and this was just what the doctor ordered.

"Come on Ma! It's already 5:00 AM," she stated while rolling her eyes. "I thought you said we were going to be on the road by 5:00 AM."

25

"I'm ready. Let's roll."

To give her and her five friends a little independence, I agreed for them to drive themselves, but I would follow behind in my own car. Looking back on that, we should have flown.

The warm breeze was inviting as we pulled into our hotel parking lot. I exhaled for two reasons. I was grateful that we made it to our destination safely, and secondly, I was preparing for my Zen experience. The girls went to check in while I stayed in the car to surveil the premises. All of a sudden, they all came out of the receptionist area looking rather puzzled.

I stuck my head out of the car and asked, "What's wrong?"

"They won't let us check in."

"WHAT?!" "Why not?" I demanded to know. The mother lioness was beginning to rise up.

I got out of the car and charged inside to talk with the receptionist.

"Hi. My daughter tells me that they can't check in. They have pre-paid for the room!"

"Yes ma'am but they are only 18 years old. Occupants must be 25 years old to stay here," the nice lady stated.

The protective mother in me turned into the playground schoolgirl who wanted to start singing, "I told you so! I told you so!" Instead, I gave my daughter *"the look." You know, the one that says,* "Well, well, well. It's a good thing I came along, huh?"

Preparing a Fruitful Harvest

As the five girls backed away from the registration desk, I got my wallet out to give the lady my ID. It was quiet for the next three minutes.

"Thank you Mrs. Prather. Your rooms are located just down the breezeway."

We all walked outside and back to our respective cars in silence. I called my daughter over to my car. "So, you know you would be up the creek if I wasn't here, right?"

"Yes, I know. Thank you."

I walked to my own room, proud and even more confident that my helicopter hovering had kept my daughter safe. *Ahhh. Relax. Relate. Release.* I finally got some much-needed self-care and sun. While watching the waves crash into the shore, I received a phone call. One of my daughter's friends' mother called to check in with me about how things were going. I assured her that all was well; I had given the girls their marching orders and I promised I'd see that her daughter got back home safely. She admitted to me that she was genuinely concerned about them going by themselves but was not as courageous as me to step in and provide a solution. She thanked me for shadowing the girls. Yes, I am a proud, hovering "helicopter mom."

When we returned home, I asked my daughter how she thought everything turned out with me being there.

"When you first told me that was the only way I could go, I was upset and felt like I couldn't do anything by myself," my daughter said.

I totally expected that. The attitude prior to the trip confirmed this.

"But in the end, it was worth it. We had a really good time. You weren't all in our business and you were cute on the beach, too. Glad we did it," she concluded.

I smiled. I was happy to hear that, because the benefit of being a helicopter mom is that your children understand that your ultimate goal is to protect them as long as you can.

What kind of mom are you or do you want to be?

Helicopter (Caring) Mom

A helicopter mom is a mother who hovers over her children while paying extremely close attention to all of the child's endeavors—academic and social. It can also be known as a "caring" mom. I think I would rather use this word instead. The connotation is much more positive. The goal of the caring mom is to spare her children the mistakes she made at their age and to be an intricate part of their lives for many years to come.

This kind of mom gets a lot of flack for obvious reasons. She seems really obsessive and controlling. Her children may feel smothered and consumed by her relentless efforts to know all and be involved in every corner of their lives. She may also be really pushy—to the point where the children may resent her tactics. Children of helicopter moms are constantly wondering if they measure up to her big expectations.

On the flip side, this kind of mom will work tirelessly to bring out her child's best qualities. The helicopter mom will be the first to recognize her child's strengths and place her child in environments that enhance these qualities. She will also be there to provide the cushion for when her children fall, providing ultimate protection for her children, right? Well, not necessarily. There has to be a healthy balance of teaching independence and confidence in our young girls while they still feel supported. We simply want to ensure our child's well-being and we want what is best for them. I recently asked another hovering mother her reason for being the kind of mother that she is. She said she just wants her child to succeed. She lamented the fact that her mother was not the guiding light she needed her to be which has caused some major hardships in her life.

Free-spirited Mom

Are you a free-spirited mom? If so, then you believe that the actions of the helicopter—or "caring mom"—deprive children of life's most precious and valuable lessons. You have high hopes, dreams and aspirations for your child, but you are aware that you are merely a guide holding their hand along this journey. To you, there is nothing else that tops your goal of self-discovery for your children, not even completing homework and making good grades.

This type of mother wants a healthy balance. Oftentimes, their own mothers or the other parents in the household are the total opposite of this free style of parenting.

Free-spirited moms want their children to be free, independent in thought, and to speak up for themselves. They want them to use their voices to effect change. One free-spirited mom explained that her children are encouraged to come to her with anything and everything. Sometimes, this means she may get a little too much information. She feels that because everyone has their own lives to live, experiences to gain, and mistakes to make, the free-spirited mom has cultivated an environment where children have no fear of judgment.

However, one of the drawbacks to this parenting style is a lack of structure and unconsidered consequences. The mother is free; thus the child is free, often putting important things aside.

Generous Mom

A generous mom prides herself on periodically indulging her children more than she knows she should, but she just can't help it! She's the fun mom who wants to make sure her children have a wonderfully happy childhood that they can reminisce and boast about well into their golden years. A generous mom also affords her child all of the opportunities that she may have missed during her heydays.

One generous mom shared that her dream was to give her children everything she didn't have. I can definitely relate to this. When my daughter reached milestone birthdays of 13, 16, and 18, I wanted to make sure we marked the occasions in ways that were memorable.

Preparing a Fruitful Harvest

For her 13th birthday, I called her entire cheer squad and asked them to meet at a local event center to surprise her. I never had a surprise party, so I wanted to make sure my daughter had one. The anticipation and excitement were intense as we were waiting for Sydnei to arrive with one of her cheer friends. We were all waiting in the dark room and as soon as she came in, we yelled "SURPRISE!!" It was the best feeling, knowing that she was getting to experience something I never did.

For her 16th birthday, we sent out invitations to over 150 of her childhood and school friends for an all-white, Sweet 16 soiree at one of the most popular party venues in the city. It was catered with an all-white candy bar and the DJ played all of the latest hits. Having a themed party was super neat. I enjoyed seeing the guests in all white dancing to the music. It reminded me of something out of a reality TV series.

Picture this: a mansion; an olympic-sized pool; jacuzzi; and the perfect summer weather. It was Sydnei's 18th birthday. I had given her some kind of party for the past 17 years, and since this was the last milestone in her teens, I wanted to make sure it was a good one. It was as if we had rented out our own little island in the city. It was the summer's hottest gig.

Another generous mom said it best. "It's clear that we are all about reward, extravagant memories, and allowed freedoms. As long as the children are deserving of it and are appreciative of these privileges, generous moms see nothing wrong with indulging their children."

Determined Mom

A determined mom is almost as extreme as the helicopter mom. In fact, you could be compared to a "tiger mom." You know, the ones who push and pressure their children to reach high levels of achievement in academics, and to be involved in extracurricular activities that hold a significant status in the community? Your goal is to frame the world as a demanding place that does not care for coddled children. You believe that coddling your children only makes them unprepared for the rough terrain ahead. Your hope is that your children will aspire to greatness and not settle for mediocrity. Life is a one-time shot, and you are determined to help them make it count. In some cases, determined mothers grew up with only one parent in the household and vowed that their children would never experience the lack they experienced as a child.

The determined mom pushes herself in order to show her children that life is not a rehearsal. It's the real thing and you should never give up on yourself or your dreams. The drive, as well as the struggles that the determined mom presents to her daughter, allow her to be fully equipped to strive for excellence in all things. However, this style of parenting comes down hard on the child, especially when the mom's expectations are not met. For example, if the child does not finish college or secure the type of job the mother expects, then the determined mom may feel a sense of failure.

Understanding your individual parenting style is important because it gives you an opportunity to assess your-

Preparing a Fruitful Harvest

self. Now that you know your style, seek to understand it better. Find out how your style will impact your relationship with your daughter, the pros and cons of your style, and how to balance it to develop a fruitful daughter. On the next page, you will complete the "7 Why's" activity to discover the root cause of why you exhibit your parenting style. When I took this test, it revealed questions I had never considered and triggered some emotions as to why I am a helicopter mom. I discovered that I am a helicopter mom because I don't want my children to fall victim to the streets.

In my experience, without the watchful eye of adults, children made poor, life-altering decisions. I didn't realize it, but because of what I witnessed, I believed that giving children too much space would result in substance abuse and jail time. I know! That seems extreme, right? But I have seen this happen in my own family, unfortunately.

The 7 Why's

Try the 7 Why's activity below. It is a technique of asking the question "Why?" to get to the root cause of a particular situation or problem. Each answer forms the basis of the next question. Keep asking "why?" until you've exhausted all conclusions or once you've arrived at your core answer.

What kind of parenting style do you practice?
___
___
___
___

Why?
___
___
___
___

Why?
___
___
___
___

Why?
___
___
___
___

Why?

_____
_____
_____

Why?

_____
_____
_____

Why?

_____
_____
_____

Why?

_____
_____
_____

What is the core reason for your parenting style?

_____
_____
_____

The ABCD's of Motherhood

Accentuate your strengths. I tend to be my own worst critic—from the way I look, to my parenting skills, to my chosen career. First of all, you should know that your strength is in your ability to bring forth life, whether naturally or surgically. I experienced both ways, and they are equally significant in the birthing process. We should own that strength and use it to cultivate change in our own lives in order to be better versions of ourselves.

Unfortunately, a manual is not provided when we become mothers. We only know what we've been taught by our own mothers or mother-figures, be it good or bad. We can learn how to be better mothers by reading and researching, as I talk about in my introduction. Also, we have our village to lean on which is a huge, under-used source of strength. Use them!! Allow them to take care of you when needed. That is a strength!

The strength of a woman lies in going on a journey to discovering just who you are as a person. Are you living a life of integrity? Are you resilient or a survivor? Accentuating these strengths gives you a purpose to live up to your highest potential. On this journey, you must give yourself grace and have patience to walk your path. You may not know who you are yet, and that's okay. Keep moving forward to finding and emphasizing those strengths.

Preparing a Fruitful Harvest

Be your own advocate. This actually started during my prenatal care, through the delivery, and especially post-delivery. My mother used to always tell me that no one will take care of you like you so SPEAK UP!! When those parenting instincts kicked in, and I knew something was not quite right with me or with my daughter, I spoke up. While we were still in the hospital, about one day after she was born, I noticed that she would shake when she cried. I immediately brought this to the attention of the nurse, and they took her to run some tests. Turns out, her glucose levels were low, so they had to supplement with formula. It was scary! But I am glad I was able to get it taken care of. Never underestimate your gut feelings.

As mothers, we must also raise our voices for causes that affect our children's education and overall health. Strength also comes in knowing when to fight and when to surrender for the greater good. We can be amazing advocates for like-minded mothers as well.

Create your own lane of impact. This is my favorite one because my purpose is to serve others. I also aspire to inspire and can do so from a woman's and a mother's point of view. We hold so many wonderful gems of wisdom that have been passed down from generation to generation. We must share our knowledge with others because I believe that informed women inform women.

By trial and error, we have the credibility to be influencers and mentors to younger generations of mothers. I get goosebumps when my cousin, who is expecting baby #2 soon, calls and asks motherhood questions of me. I am encouraged and honored by her confidence in me to steer her onto the right path. Mothers must be impactful by educating and equipping other mothers to take care of themselves. It teaches their daughters the art of self-care as well. We must do the work of finding out more of what makes younger mothers come alive and mobilize that vision to help other moms.

Demand your worth. Personally, this was a hard one for me. As a single mother, I wasn't aware of my worth. I was worried about being a statistic and the stigma that came along with being an unwed mother. It took me a very long time to understand that dysfunction was not functional. I had to learn my worth and then demand it. Among other things, my worth included areas of respect, support, consistency, communication, and commitment. I am worthy of these things in order to be the best mother I can be.

There is no way to be a perfect mother, but there are hundreds of ways to be a good one. Use the *ABCD's of Motherhood* as an empowerment tool in answering the call to show up for yourselves. We must remember that we had lives of our own with dreams and passions before we had children. Let's never forget!

Preparing a Fruitful Harvest

Complete the activity below.

Accentuate Your Strengths: Write your top 5 strengths as a woman and/or as a mother.

Woman: Mother:

_____   _____

_____   _____

_____   _____

_____   _____

_____   _____

How do these strengths improve your life and the lives of your family members?

_____
_____
_____
_____

Be Your Own Advocate:

Are you in a situation now where you need an advocate? If so, what is that situation?

_____
_____
_____
_____

How would you want an advocate to help you?
_____
_____
_____
_____

How can you be that same advocate for yourself?
_____
_____
_____
_____

Create Your Own Lane of Impact:

What are some of the needs of your tribe or circle?
_____
_____
_____
_____

Are you willing to lead the community to address those needs?
_____
_____
_____
_____

How can you help other mothers or women be the best version of themselves?
_____
_____
_____
_____

Demand Your Worth:

What is stopping you from realizing your worth?
_____
_____
_____
_____

How can you overcome those barriers?
_____
_____
_____
_____

What is one way you will demand your worth from this day forward?
_____
_____
_____
_____

The Viable Village

The old African proverb, "It takes a village to raise a child," is literally what has sustained me for the past 21 years. The grandparents, girlfriends, aunties, god-mamas and play mamas have come to my rescue more times than I can count. As a young, single mother, sorority sisters were the glue when I became unglued with the mounting responsibilities of motherhood. Free babysitters, like my parents, allowed me to take a few classes in pursuit of my master's degree. It is important that you cultivate and appreciate your village, as you will need them to strengthen you on this journey.

The viable village is the group of close-knit, selfless individuals who help mothers be the best for their children and for themselves. Usually, these are the people who have been in your life for quite some time, who know you and your personality well, and who have been given the authority to hold you accountable. These are the people who don't wait to be asked if they can help. They just do it because they see the need, especially if mom is too busy—or too stubborn—to ask for the help.

It is especially important for you to take care of your mental health, especially after childbirth. Postpartum depression or the "baby blues" is not something to be taken lightly. It is a complication of giving birth and in no way means you are a bad mother. A strong and viable village can be there to help you cope with overwhelming feelings of sadness, mood swings, crying—the typical baby blues. However, if you're showing signs of hopelessness, or severe panic and anxiety attacks, you may be dealing with postpartum depression which requires immediate medical assistance. Your viable village can assist with getting the professional help you need.

Rely on your village for physical support. I remember when I could not pick up my daughter from afterschool care one day due to work obligations. If I weren't there by 6:00 PM, I would have been charged a dollar per minute after the grace period of five minutes. The way my day was going, I was going to be late.

"Hey girl! I have a dilemma. Can you get Syd by 6:00 PM today? I am so sorry for the late notice, but I am stuck at work until at least 7:00 PM." I asked my best friend, Jasmine.

"Let me check to make sure I am able to leave in time." After about a minute, she came back to the phone and said, "I got you. Don't worry. Do you want me to get her something to eat as well?"

"You're a lifesaver. Yes, please get her something to eat and I'll pay you back when I pick her up. Should be no later than 8:00 PM", I said with relief.

"Girl, bye! You know you don't have to pay me back. See you soon and be careful," Jasmine said, laughing.

Your village should possess the A.I.D.E. factor. After all, that is what they are called to do—help you like an aide would. They are to:

A – Assist you with anything and everything. This could be cooking meals, helping you plan and execute milestone events such as birthdays and graduations, and supporting your child in the school play or cheer competition. Also, they should be the sounding board for when you need to vent about things.

I – Insist upon you taking some time for yourself. Self-care is particularly important for mothers, no matter if you're a stay-at-home mom, work-from-home mom, or if you work outside the home. This is discussed in detail in the next chapter.

D – Develop with the times. Make sure they are staying abreast of our ever-changing world of technology, jargon, and all of the things that are important to young people today. This way, they may be able to talk with your teenager who is not comfortable confiding in you.

E – Energize you and vice versa. Pour life into each other so that the village is filled up as well. Moms, we have a unique opportunity to always give our village their flowers while they are still around to smell them because they play such an important role in our lives.

The viable village should be made up of those people in whom you have complete confidence. You should be able to trust them with your life and your child's life. The village should also hold the same values and virtues that you hold as a mother. Such strengths should include being responsible, attentive, patient, full of tough love and devoted to the success of you and your child's future.

Preparing a Fruitful Harvest

Although I talk about family members being a part of the village, please note that biology is not a requirement to be in the village. Sometimes, your own family cannot be a part of your village and that's okay. Blood is the least of what makes some people your "family." Be intentional about seeking out your village. Watch how that village takes care of you and your child(ren) for years to come, oftentimes offering up assistance to your college student when you don't even know it and you don't even have to ask. That's the love of the village I call family.

Self-Care

"A mother who radiates self-love and self-acceptance actually vaccinates her daughter against low self-esteem."
- Naomi Wolf

    Mothers, knowingly or unknowingly, teach their daughters how to treat themselves. Mothers are a young girl's first role model. What she sees in mom ultimately shapes her reality. Therefore, it is important that daughters see their mothers practice self-care, as this will ensure the daughters are more inclined to do the same.
    Self-care has gained notoriety in recent years for good reason. With the hustle and bustle of life, and especially now, during this COVID-19 pandemic, women in general, and mothers especially, cannot afford to put self-care on the back burner. We need all hands on deck, firing on all cylinders, and all elevators going to the top floor!
    Self-care is literally taking a time out—just for you, to love yourself. Many women feel guilty even thinking about caring for themselves. They believe it is selfish and that they don't deserve it. When I was a young single mother, I battled with this guilt. I felt like my daughter deserved all of my attention. I felt like I had to make up for the time I spent at work and the time she didn't get with her biological father. I felt like spending money on myself was somehow taking money from my daughter. The idea of spending time away from her felt like selfish vanity.

Preparing a Fruitful Harvest

As I matured as a mother, and with the help of my viable village, I was able to realize that self-care is very personal and unselfish. It's actually selfless. In fact, it would be selfish if I *did not* take time to rejuvenate my mind, body, and spirit because I would be depriving my loved ones of receiving the best version of me. I realized that even though I was with my daughter, she was not getting the best of me. I was tired, frustrated, afraid, and uncared for. How could I care for her when I didn't know what care really meant? I was empty, and I could not pour from an empty vessel.

Feeling frustrated and angry due to always working and being the sole provider for my daughter, I found myself lashing out at others, including my own mother. That is something that I never wanted to do and she didn't raise me that way. One day, she told me.

"A!" This was my mother's nickname for me.

"A! No one will take care of you like you."

Yeah, whatever, I thought. I was angry and brushed her words of wisdom off for about a week. Those words began to replay in my mind. I began to understand just what she was saying to me. I had to find a way to control my outbursts and breakdowns. What was I going to do about it? I thought that maybe I needed to see my doctor or a psychologist at first. I felt like I was having a nervous breakdown. But when I sat down and really thought about it, I realized that all I wanted was some time to take care of myself and my needs.

The next day, I wrote out a wish-list of things I'd like to do for myself each week. The first week, I would read one of the many books sitting on the shelf collecting dust. The next week, I would go for a mani/pedi as I didn't often get those at the same time. The week after, I would schedule a facial to combat some acne I was experiencing, which was probably from the stress of it all. I decided to make this a part of my monthly regimen. These little escapes did wonders for my soul and I thought, *WOW! Where has this been all my life?* It really wasn't hard to steal away one to two hours a week just to do me, and my child probably appreciated the break as well.

Starting out, I would indulge in these mini spa days as often as I could because they made me feel good, refreshed, and sexy. Over the years, as I've learned more and more about self-care, it has become clear that proper self-care is a total mind, body, and soul experience. Salt baths, stay-cations, or eating your favorite dessert are all great things to do for yourself. But let's go deeper to really engage ourselves at the highest level. I've learned that getting proper medical care is an essential part of self-care. Also, setting boundaries with family and friends is self-care. If you know that being around certain people brings you down, avoiding them is self-care, even if it makes them angry.

Self-care is anything that brings you peace, fulfillment, and happiness. It is designed for you to be in complete control, and you get to decide how self-care looks and feels for you. Just remember, it may involve a little sacri-

Preparing a Fruitful Harvest

fice. One such sacrifice may be waking up 30 minutes earlier or going to bed 30 minutes later. Use this time to write out your plans for the next 12-24 hours. You don't have to buy a fancy journal or anything. A plain piece of paper or notebook will do just fine. Write at the top of the page "THINGS TO DO" and list everything you want to get done. Examples could include answering old emails, calling a relative, paying a certain bill, etc. Make it as specific as possible. Once you complete a task, mark it off your list. This gives an immediate sense of accomplishment and gratification.

Consider repeating positive affirmations to yourself throughout the day, or better yet, while you're brushing your teeth in the morning. This is a great habit to start, and attaching it to a daily task will help you remember to do it. Positive affirmations are complete sentences that can start with "I," "I am," or "I will," and state your intent for your health and wellness or your dreams for the future. Positive affirmations can be recited at any time of the day or night, especially when you may be feeling unproductive, unmotivated, or unsure of yourself. However, it's very important to only focus on the positive (what you want) instead of the negative (what you don't want).

Say this: "I am healthy" instead of, "I don't want to be sick." Saying what you want to have happen activates its journey to you. Likewise, saying the opposite of what you want also activates its journey to you, so choose your words wisely. My favorite positive affirmation is, "I am healthy, wealthy and wise. I am authentic, free, and graceful. I am right where I am supposed to be and walking in my purpose of serving others." This sets the tone for my day and allows me to flow in the energy of positivity and creates a life inclusive of all I've stated.

As a mom, we can use positive affirmations to help us plant the seeds to reap a fruitful harvest in our daughters. Here are four, to start off:

1. I am raising a positive, prepared, and productive citizen of this world.

2. I model self-respect, self-worth, and self-awareness to my daughter.

3. I am thoughtful in my communication with my daughter.

All generational cycles end with me.

Self-care can also be anything that creates an escape for you, such as a 15-minute walk around the block. Walking is a natural mood-booster and helps to combat depression. A monthly massage appointment to loosen those knots in your back, neck and shoulders can ease anxiety. Even cooking a healthy meal that your body will thank you for is good self-care because food is medicine.

Self-care can also look like listening to your favorite music station in the car on the way to work and belting out a tune or two. Music is healing. Notice your mood shifts when your jam comes on. Suddenly, you're smiling and bobbing your head to the beat. Those feel-good endorphins have been activated.

One of my favorite self-care treats is taking a long, hot shower, envisioning the steamy waterfall melting away

Preparing a Fruitful Harvest

the stress and strain of the day and all of the negativities being washed down the drain. I also like to get dolled up, put on some nice clothes, do my make-up and take selfies that may or may not get posted to social media. That's self-love on display!

Resting is an essential part of self-care. Proper rest, in today's environment, is really unheard of because the world expects us to go and keep going like Energizer bunnies. Is resting considered laziness? Of course not, but there was a point in time that I thought I was being lazy while just vegging out on the couch.

I had a lot of guilt and shame for doing something so essential to our souls. Resting provides overall health benefits like rejuvenating your mind to handle all of the different aspects of your life. Your cells get a recharge. Mothers have to take extra special care to rest. But with the demands of family and work, what is the best way? Below are some of the ways busy moms can get in some rest.

Guided meditation. There are tons of tutorials on YouTube as well as many apps you can use to help with guided breaths and focused attention. Repeating your favorite positive affirmations goes well with meditating.

Spiritual bath. It's definitely different from a normal bath or shower that you may take every day. It's a ritualistic cleansing to calm the mind and relax the body. The goal is to soak in the positive energy from the water by adding salts, essential oils, flowers, and dried herbs. You can also place candles and crystals around the tub for a better spiritual experience so that negative energy is removed, revealing a renewed sense of being.

Saying no to social engagements to stay home to rest is perfectly okay. There is nothing wrong with putting your comfort and mental health first.

My mother once told me, "If you look good, you feel good." Self-care is taking that one step further. If you feel good, then you'll do good! A mother has to be filled up in order to run her household effectively. If mama is not okay, NOBODY is okay. We deserve the same care and concern we so easily bestow upon others. No one else is responsible for your happiness. No one else can take care of you like you can.

Complete the activity below:

Fitness: If you take care of your mind, the body will follow. Consider getting more exercise, adopting a healthier diet, seeking therapy, or taking yoga. What are your total fitness goals?

_____
_____
_____
_____

Family: Consider starting new traditions, defining ways to create generational wealth and health, or being more community-focused. What major breakthroughs can your family have today?

___

Faith: Faith is activated by God. Fear is activated by the enemy. Consider overcoming your fears by going for that dream job or start that business or writing that book. How does your spirituality affect your goals?

___

Finances: Consider budget creation, savings, additional streams of income, home ownership and going back to school for additional training. What's your financial story and how does it allow you to reach your goals?

___

Fun: Work hard and play harder, right? Consider brunching with friends, taking a solo trip, skydiving, learning a new skill or hobby, reading more, and just celebrating the small wins. How do you want to spend your free time?

_____
_____
_____
_____

V.I.S.I.O.N.

Vision is the ability to imagine a future that you get to design. As mothers, we often overlook our vision because we are so enthralled in the throes of motherhood. But pursuing your vision is a part of the self-care I talked about earlier. You must be in control of your thoughts, which create your destiny. It's never too late to make a plan for the life you want to live, as a woman and as a mother.

I do an annual vision board and women's empowerment workshop for the New Year. Use the following acronym to develop the proper mindset around creating your personal and professional goals.

Visualize – Do you have dreams of walking the red carpet in an Alexander McQueen custom-made gown like Michelle Obama at a White House gala? Do you desire to drive a pewter, plush, Mercedes-Maybach GLS 600 4Matic on a random shopping spree on Rodeo Drive? Want to write a check for $1 million to your favorite charity and not miss it? What about building a boarding house for women and girls who are victims of domestic abuse? Close your eyes and imagine yourself going to that place, doing those things, and being that person you've always dreamed of being. See it with your spirit's eye. Make sure you feel those feelings. Sit in that moment. It's hard to be what you cannot see. Repeat several times a week.

Intentionality – Mindfulness and being present in the moment are, unfortunately, lost arts. Smartphones and social media have pulled us away from being deliberate in our pursuits. We live in a society of the microwave mentality and quick fixes, but cultivating your vision requires your resolute attention to detail. That means it will take some time to craft. Use that time wisely by investing in yourself and your craft. You must stay mindful of the end goal.

Speak It – Are you aware that you are energy and what you emit out into the universe comes right back to you? Your lips dictate your life. What you think and say about yourself is true. Life and death are in the power of the tongue, so speak those positive affirmations we explored in Section 1. Start saying: "I am a great mother" or whatever your vision may be. This is an intentional practice of faith.

Ignite It – The Bible states that in the beginning, God said, "Let there be light." Even scientists who deny the existence of God capitulate to the fact that in an instance, the beginning of time began with a "big boom" – a huge explosion of extreme light. When God began His creation, He had to ignite an explosive force of energy. Likewise, you cannot be passive about your vision; you must be ignited into action with an explosion of energy.

Own your Shine – This dark world needs your light. Have you ever tried to dumb down yourself because you didn't want to seem too confident or charismatic, too smart or happy? It feels unnatural and off-balance because you are blessed to be a blessing, not to be a conduit for the insecurities of others. Own who you are–all of your quirkiness and cuteness! You are destined to do great things in this life.

"<u>N</u>O!" – This one word has the power to change your entire life. It is a complete sentence with no explanation needed. The journey to your vision should be devoid of barriers that delay you getting to your destination. These barriers could be family, friends, or negative mindsets. Clear boundaries should be set to minimize distractions. You must say "NO" to anything that doesn't get you closer to your vision. Remember, saying yes to one thing means you are saying no to something else. Your life goals should not be the sacrificial lamb.

Creating your V.I.S.I.O.N. is generational health in action. It sets your mind on a path to leaving a legacy for your daughter, ultimately planting seeds of determination in her. She is watching you for guidance on what it looks like to go after your dreams and goals, so be very diligent to incorporate this six-part acronym.

Mama, You're Doing a Great Job!

Socrates said, "Envy is the ulcer of the soul." *Ouch!!* This is true, however, because it causes us to miss our own joyful moments—moments that we can never get back. However, the urge to compare is so strong because, well, it is human nature. It causes us to look within and deal with our own low self-image, insecurities, and shortcomings. I confess I was envious of a mom once. We worked together at a local insurance company and were pregnant at the same time. Our daughters were born a week apart.

While on maternity leave, there was one particular day that I was having an especially hard time. It was October of 1999 and Sydnei was just three months old. I remember thinking, "I can't do this. It's too hard. I am failing her." She was my first baby, and I had no clue of what to do, really.

"Why is she crying like this?" I asked my mother, as I cried too. "She doesn't like me."

"Maybe she has gas," my mom said as she laid her down on the bed and gently pushed her knees into her chest. Suddenly, popping noises were coming from her bottom and her crying subsided.

"Yep! She just has gas, girl, and yes, she likes you. Stop that!" my mother said matter-of-factly.

In the heat of the moment, it did not occur to me that all of this crying was normal, and that my daughter was just doing her little job of alerting me so that I could do my big job of tending to her. It wasn't going to permanently scar her to cry or to be a little inconvenienced. My mother reminded me that I am Sydnei's world, and there was nothing I could do—that she would remember anyway—that could change that. Still, it was nerve-wracking, and I was a mess!

Soon after, I decided to run to the grocery store to get some gas drops so that her little tummy could get some added relief. As I approached the entrance, I saw my co-worker, a fellow pregnancy pal, in the grocery store. It was a pretty, fall Saturday morning and I noticed her hair was freshly and professionally styled and her postpartum body was snatched to the gods. Geez! It had only been three months.

She wore a nice, form-fitting sundress with some chucks with a light and natural face beat. To me, she looked very relaxed, refreshed, and rejuvenated. I hadn't seen her since the last day of working before we both went out on maternity leave. We were actually due to start back in the office that following Monday. She seemed so well put together, even on this random store run.

"Dang! She is winning at this motherhood thing." I thought. On the contrary, I had thrown on some yoga pants, a tunic top, put on a baseball cap, some lip oil and slid my feet into some comfortable crocs. My eyes were still a little puffy from the crying episode I just had due to the unrelenting gas bubbles in my baby's stomach. Luckily, we didn't get a chance to talk to each other at the store as she was going in the opposite direction as me. I really didn't want her to see me like this.

Monday morning came pretty fast. It was our first day back from maternity leave. I surely didn't want to be there, but as they say, "Time to make the donuts." I saw my pregnancy pal and I decided to ask her to share her secret to conquering motherhood. "Hey lady! How was your maternity leave? I saw you at Kroger on Saturday and you looked fab. Sorry we didn't get to chat, but I wanted to ask you, what's your new mom secret?"

"Girl, it was good, but I wished I had more help. I didn't get any breaks and I didn't want to leave her today, you know? I am nervous about her being at daycare. But I am glad I found someone who will take good care of her while I work. As you know, I don't have any real family here. Everyone is up north in the Chicago area.

I had to take her with me to get my hair and nails done for this first day back at work. I don't have any secrets, girl! I'm just trying to make it day by day. Sometimes, hour by hour. I go out of my way to fix myself up and working out is a good way to keep postpartum depression at bay. I am so exhausted, and I don't think I am winning at this motherhood thing, so looking good makes me feel good about myself," she said with a look of desperation on her face. "So, how was maternity leave for you?"

"Ummm... it was great, actually. I haven't been able to work out like I want to yet, but my mom and grandmother were there to help with a lot of things," I said with a little bit of caution because I was coming into an eye-opening realization about perception versus reality.

Preparing a Fruitful Harvest

She continued. "WOW! You are truly blessed. You had help from your mom and grandma—basically your village was there! I would have loved to have someone there for me during those hard times or just to sleep in. You seem to have it all together. You are always so calm, cool, and collected. Probably because you were able to get some good sleep, LOL!!"

Wait. Did she just say she thinks I have it all together? I thought to myself.

"Well, thank you. I think we are all just doing the best we can, and I am sure you are doing a great job, mama."

This taught me some valuable lessons about being envious of others. Simply put, there's no use. Life is cyclical and we all have our times of lack and times of abundance. I was able to work through these issues by remembering the infamous words my late mother once told me:

"Everybody has issues. Either they are in a storm, coming out of a storm, or about to go into a storm. The good news is that everything is temporary."

I still use this mantra today in all aspects of my life. You just never, ever know what someone is going through, so always be kind to others. Never assume anything. Things are not always as they appear to be and what you consider inferiority, someone else may consider superiority. Life and parenting are ever evolving. As long as you are doing your best for your child and are taking care of her needs, you are doing a great job, mama!

Prepare the Planter

What is your parenting style and why?
_____
_____
_____
_____

Upon which letter of the *ABCD's of Motherhood* can you improve?
_____
_____
_____
_____

Do you have a viable village? If so, how do they support you? If not, what steps will you take to choose your village?
_____
_____
_____
_____

How will you show up and take better care of yourself?
_____
_____
_____
_____

Preparing a Fruitful Harvest

What's your V.I.S.I.O.N.? How does outlining your path help to create generational health for your daughter?

_____
_____
_____
_____

Section 2
Preparing the Soil

Breaking Generational Cycles

When I was younger, there were definitely some things that I said I would do, would not do, allow, or not allow when I had my own family. There was a certain way I wanted my home life to feel: safe, secure, peaceful, full of laughter—a sanctuary of forgiveness, faith, hope and love. However, being a single mother brought many challenges, and I found myself living the exact opposite of what I wanted. Instead of safety and security, I was living in fear, angst, and worry. Instead of laughter, I was stressed and lashing out. Instead of forgiveness, I was angry and bitter. Over time, I realized that I had been perpetuating dysfunctional generational cycles which were stopping me from being the mother I longed to be.

Before you can plant any seeds, you must prepare the soil. Tilling the soil means breaking up the old ground which has been settled over years. In the old dirt, you find rocks, weeds, fungus, and other harmful elements which will choke out your new seeds. You literally have to dig up and disturb the roots. You have to create a healthy environment where your seeds will be nourished and will thrive. In this section of the book, we will discuss the hardened grounds in our lives: our negative generational cycles.

The cycles we will address are communication, fear, and lack of therapy. It is never too late to start new habits, beliefs, and behaviors in our mother/daughter experience. The choices of our parents do not have to be our own.

Love Languages

"I love you," "Love ya," "Love you lots," "Love you more." These words were never spoken in my home as a child. No one said them so I didn't feel left out or unloved or anything. It was just something we didn't do as a family. I knew love was present. Without a doubt, I knew I was loved. Now, I am not suggesting that saying "I love you" is the be-all and end-all to a healthy family unit. There are many ways to say it, show it, prove it, and do it. I heard my friends' parents and siblings emoting these words freely among each other, and I wondered "Well, what's up with us not saying it?"

Think about that. I grew up in an environment where the words "I love you" were never uttered, but somehow, I felt the void of the words. If you never tasted ice cream, would you desire the taste of ice cream? Most likely not. Yet, I longed to hear the words "I love you" though I had never tasted the sweetness of the words. Love is not a cultural or environmental thing; it is a biological and psychological necessity that is just as important to the healthy development of a person as are food and water. Of course, I'm not suggesting a person would die if they didn't hear or feel love for a few days, like one could if they were to go without food and water, but I do believe a lifetime without some form of love could kill the spirit.

As I grew older, I came to understand the expressions of love. Sure, my mom never said the words, but I learned why after reading Gary Chapman's *The Five Love Languages*. From this highly recommended book, I learned that love is expressed in different ways. A love language is just that—it is the language in which people express love. Love languages are not inherited or assimilated like diction. A child can be born with a love language that is completely opposite from her mother's. Without this knowledge, a mother and daughter may never speak or understand each other's love language. Can you imagine giving birth to a child, speaking English to them, and when they speak their first words, the words come out in French? Well, this happens more often than you would believe, and many families have suffered because they did not understand they were speaking a foreign love language.

According to Chapman, the 5 Love Languages are:

Words of affirmation: A person who feels and shares love with words of love and affirmation.

Quality time: A person who needs undisturbed quality time with a loved one to feel loved.

Receiving gifts: A person who feels and shows love by giving and receiving gifts.

Acts of service: A person who feels and shows love by what they do for a person or what a person does for them.

Physical touch: A person who feels and shares love through physical touch.

My mother's primary love language was "gifts." She loved to give gifts. She loved to see other people's expressions and it delighted her to be able to make them happy in that way. My love language, however, is words of affirmation. I want to hear your feelings and as such, I wanted to understand why it was so hard for my family to say those three words. My language does not comprehend gifts, and a person who needs gifts does not comprehend words.

The "Gifter" says to the "Talker," "You keep *saying* you love me, but I can't tell because you never show it. You never get me anything."

The "Talker" says to the "Gifter," "You can keep all of these gifts. Tell me you love me. Tell me you missed me today."

These two never feel loved by the other, even though they are both giving all the love they have. They are speaking a foreign language with no interpreter. As mothers, we have to identify the love language of our daughters, so as to speak their language.

You Must Speak Your Daughter's Love Language, Not Your Own

Don't be stubborn about your love language. The most common and destructive mindset we have when showing love is the mindset of, "This is just how I am. I can't help it." You can and you must help it.

Confucius once said, "The man who thinks he can and the man who thinks he can't are both right." I strongly believe in the creative power of thoughts and words, so if you are constantly saying or thinking that you can't be better or show love in a way that your daughter needs, then you won't. You have to do the work of consistently feeding your mind the positives and make decisions that are going to be fruitful to the kind of life you want to live and the kind of example you want your daughter to see. It's your life now—not your parents' or grandparents'.

If you were to visit China for a month, would you not take a translation book so that you could better understand the language and surroundings? Would you not attempt to learn the basic communications like, "Thank you" and "Please?" You absolutely would because your ability to survive in that environment depends on your understanding of the language. Love is the nutrient of a fruitful harvest and it is needed to survive.

You may not *feel* the satisfaction of speaking your daughter's love language, but that doesn't mean that your efforts are insincere. As I stated before, my mother lit up like a lightbulb when she gave gifts. She was expressing love in her purest state. She would not have felt that same excitement *saying* the words I love you, but it would have meant the world to me. Likewise, if your language is different from your daughter's, you may not get the same enthusiasm and fulfilling emotion by speaking her language, but you must learn to find the greater satisfaction that you are giving your child the love she needs to flourish.

***

One day, I made up my mind that I was going to say those three words. I was determined to taste the sweet fruit of telling my mother that I loved her and hearing her say the same to me. I gathered up my courage and walked to the kitchen where my mom was washing dishes. My heart was pounding, and my temperature rose.

Am I catching a fever? I wondered.

My palms started sweating the closer I got to the den. You would have thought I was walking the Long Green Mile.

Dead girl walking!

The few feet between my room and the kitchen felt like the journey of a thousand miles. As I got closer, I saw the back of my mom's head and my legs locked up.

Um, she's busy. I'll do it another day.

No, I rebuked myself. *Do it now. What are you so afraid of? It's just three words.*

I could feel the battle between my brain and my mouth, and my brain was about to win. I was just about to turn and retreat...

Just call her name, I thought to myself. *You can't turn back then.*

"Ma!" I proclaimed.

"Yes?"

"Love you, Ma." I squeaked.

As I uttered these words, I felt a big rush, a warmness running through my body, as if I were completely embarrassed by the emotions. Why was this? Why was it so hard for me to say these three words? The speed of sound must have been broken that day, or at least it seemed like it, because it felt like the words oozed out of my mouth like extra thick molasses. My adrenaline was racing.

What is she going to say?

It seemed like an eternity in that fraction of a second.

Without turning her head from washing the dishes, she said nonchalantly, "Love you."

I didn't like that feeling at all because I wanted to *want to* say it to her. She was, after all, my mother and I wanted her to hear it. Like me, she knew she was loved even if the words were never spoken. But I kinda wish they were, ya know? I later found out why my mom never said it. It was because her mother, yes, my amazing, magical, glorious grandmother, never said those words either.

After my heroic attempt to express love, I realized that I may never hear those words come from my mother, but I told myself that when I became a mom, I would say those words, or some variation, to my children each and every day. Since this was not something that was carried out in my childhood, I wanted to make sure it was started with me. To this day, my daughter and my son hear those words as much as they hear their names.

I started a tradition of "I love you's" within my own family despite it being missing from my childhood. When we hang up the phone, when we depart from each other, when we just feel like saying it, we say it. Hopefully, by my example, my children will continue to say these words to their children, creating a legacy of health and breaking the generational cycle.

Luckily, my daughter's love language is the same as mine—words of affirmation. So after declaring that I would change this dynamic in my family, I found that saying, "I love you" worked very well with her.

Can you identify your daughter's love language?

"Mommy! I just want to be around you, climb up in your lap and cuddle with you. Give me lots of hugs please because **physical touch** is my love language."

"Mommy! Look at me! I can do the latest dance. After I shimmy across the room, can you play dress up with me because my love language is **quality time**."

"OMG Mommy! Do you really think I can dance? I just love it when you say I am the best dancer that you know. **Words of affirmation** are my love language."

"Mommy! You really surprised me at lunch today with a handwritten note attached to my peanut butter and jelly sandwich that said, 'Have a FANTABULOUS day!' That meant the world to me because my love language is **gifts**."

"Oh Mommy! Can you please make me a peanut butter and jelly sandwich? It tastes so much better when you make it. You put a little extra 'umph' in it and that makes me feel good because my love language is **acts of service**."

Your Tone Matters

The way we speak and communicate with one another is just as important as what we say. Two people can say the exact same thing but the tone in which it was stated makes all the difference in the world.

One of my favorite artists, India Arie, has a song called *The Truth* and one of her lyrics goes like this: *"How can the same man that makes me so mad (**You know what he did?**), turn right around and kiss me so soft (**Girl, you know what he did?**)."*

The first bold expression is one of hurt and anger. Imagine a scorned woman saying that to one of her girlfriends. It would be filled with attitude! The second bold expression conveys passion and tenderness, braggadocious even. She's clearly in awe and it's all in her tone because she's talking about the softness of a kiss from her love. Same words, two different tones. Parenting is no different.

For as long as I can remember, I wanted to be a mother. I think little girls start to prepare for motherhood during the toddler years. I remember getting my first doll, kitchen set, ironing board, and playhouse. I would comfort and hold my baby doll, feed her with the little pink bottles that had a white substance in them that looked like milk. I had little diapers to put on her, pretending that she had peed and pooped. This was supposed to be art imitating life, right? This was too easy. The little baby doll didn't cry, it didn't pee or poop, it stayed the same size the whole time. I could pack up my playhouse and put it in the corner until I wanted to play with it again. I could even put the baby doll down on the floor and walk away from her whenever I wanted to. I could do this!

Although playing house and being a mommy to my dolls was very innate and natural, it wasn't an accurate depiction of what real motherhood was about. As I got on up into my teenage years, I still didn't think there was much to this motherhood thing. I didn't realize how seamless my mother made taking care of us look. But I soon came to find out that motherhood is HARD!!

It is hard deciphering your baby's cries and moans. It is hard to figure out how to soothe and comfort them. It is hard dealing with the worries and heartaches during sleepless nights when they are sick. When they are toddlers, you struggle to keep up with them as their mobility makes them think they are 12 years old instead of 2 years old, and let's talk about the tween and teen years. That's where things get really interesting with a daughter, due to puberty. The hormones, mood swings, attitudes, smart mouths, back-talking, rolling of the eyes, smacking of the lips. These are the kinds of things that push moms to the brink.

I should know because I was a teenager once and was not immune to the scolding tongues of my parents. My mother also had a way of looking at me when I was out of line. I think that her uncompromising nature was intimidating to my soft-spokenness. So, when I became a mother, I wanted my voice to be heard and unfortunately, my crime was yelling. I didn't think I was yelling, however. I am a passionate person, so my words get enunciated rather purposefully and with conviction. But my daughter still says it sounds like yelling to her.

"Ma, why are you yelling? Stop yelling at me. This is not the way to get my attention." This would infuriate me because the lesson was being missed for the argument of whether I was yelling or not.

One day, when things got a bit heated, I slowed myself down and really listened to my tone and my volume. I guess you could say I was raising my voice quite loudly, which was translating as shouting and yelling to her ears. I had to own that. I had to apologize and work really hard to understand my own tone and catch myself when I wanted to go higher.

My daughter is a Leo, just like my mom. She needs to be loved, respected, and admired. She thrives off of warmth and generosity, so I wasn't serving her well with my loudness and seemingly disrespectful nature. She was not hearing me at all. I found out that this just exacerbated the situation even more and it was a lose-lose situation. Therefore, I had to learn how to speak her language when I wanted to get my point across and raising my voice was not it. I actually allowed her to lead the conversation and I matched her tone. That seemed to work for us. I later found out that the way I speak to my children is the way they will speak to their children. Children inherit those sounds we put into their ears. It became clear that healthy communication is one of the best things I could do for my daughter so that she can pass that along to her daughter, one day, as well.

In closing, check your tone, volume, and intent when speaking to your daughter. Remember that *how you say it* is just as important as what you say. Make sure your words are seasoned with grace and love. In all discourse, your goal should be to nurture, teach, and train your daughter, not harm or destroy. Try to put emphasis only on the constructive words you're speaking. Enter your conversations being solutions-driven to get to the heart of problems.

Fear

When I was growing up, the place to go in Nashville during Halloween was the Haunted Woods. It was a harrowing open field of gory and ghastly ghouls and horror movie characters like Freddy Kruger, Michael Myers and Jason, waiting to scare the bejesus out of its patrons. All of the children would come back to school after the weekend to share their experiences, and my friends and I were determined to go no matter what.

My best friends and I made our plans to get to the woods. We begged and bugged our parents until they relented. We were going to be going late and it would be after midnight before we got home, so none of our parents were willing to come get us. We were not about to let them ruin this opportunity, so we all told our parents that the parents of one of the other friends would pick us up. How were we *really* going to get back? We didn't know, and we didn't care. We would cross that bridge when we got to it. All of our classmates were going to be there—or so we thought—so we figured it would be no problem to find a ride back home.

The Haunted Woods did not disappoint. My friends and I yelled, screamed, and ran through every acre of that place. We were so excited and had so much fun, in fact, that when we started looking for a ride home, we were all alone. *Holy crap*! We were stranded in the woods! This was turning into a real-life horror story. It was 2:00 AM,

Preparing a Fruitful Harvest

pitch black outside, and the venue was closing and turning off any lights that were shining. We were about to live the first episode of Discovery Channel's *Lost and Afraid*!

There were no cell phones back then, so we needed to go to the nearest telephone booth. Unfortunately, it was about five miles down a dark, winding road. As we psyched ourselves up to take the first step, the blinding high beams of a pick-up truck came around the bend. This was our only hope. We couldn't walk down that dark road. Who knew what would have been waiting for us. Wild animals? Freddy Kruger? We were desperate.

The pick-up truck slowed down as he came closer and came to an eerie squealing stop.

"You girls need any help?" The stranger asked.

"Yes!" I spoke. My friend grabbed my arm. I'm sure she was hearing "stranger danger" alarms in her head. But I saw more danger in those dark woods.

"We need a ride to the store to make a phone call," I told him.

"Jump in," he said. We didn't realize how much danger we had put ourselves in. Luckily, we got to the store and made a phone call to a friend who came out at 2 AM to pick us up. My parents never knew this.

Knowing what I know now, I would have been livid if my daughter made the kinds of decisions I made that night. Right? It's unimaginable. It's scary. It's dangerous. I am sure my parents would have also been upset with me had they known. However, even though this happened to me and I felt terrified in the moment, I vowed to never project my own fears onto my daughter.

Sure, I would teach her to always be vigilant, and to never get into cars with strangers—although we have Uber and Lyft now. I would teach her to always be aware of her surroundings and to live by the rule, "If we come together, we leave together." You know, the Girl Code! I have to be secure in the fact that my teachings will stay with her as she matriculates through this life, and at the same time, be sure not to instill within her the paralyzing fears that I battled at her age. There are many fears we instill within our children for their safety: stranger danger, don't do drugs, drinking and driving, unprotected sex. These are topics we address with negative connotations because our goals are to scare them so thoroughly about these ideas that they will instinctively stay away from the dangers.

However, saddling your personal fears and rejections on your daughter is poison to a fruitful harvest. For example, I never applied to any other colleges except Tennessee State University, which was only 10 minutes away from my house. I toyed with applying to Spelman College, Dillard University, Howard University, and others, but I was fearful because my parents seemed fearful, especially my mom. In her subtle way, she talked me out of it.

"Are you sure you want to go *all the way* out there?" she would ask. "What if something happens? We won't be able to get to you in time." The suggestion was that being away from home almost certainly meant that I would get

Preparing a Fruitful Harvest

into some kind of trouble that I would not be able to survive due to my distance away from home. The fears that my mother projected upon me, although it came from a place of love, were destiny crushers. They hampered my sense of adventure and curiosity. I would even go so far as to say that such projection of fears stunts our growth.

Let's say I did go "all the way out there" to Atlanta, Georgia and did hit hard times. Most likely, I would have figured out how to manage the problem and thus matured mentally and emotionally. Trying to save our daughters from the things that we fear is not a help to them, it is an injury. It is akin to Munchausen Syndrome in a way.

Munchausen Syndrome is a psychological disorder and a form of child abuse. Caretakers, usually mothers, with this syndrome convince their children that they are sick. They make up symptoms, and in extreme cases, cause symptoms by poisoning their children. Is that not what we do when we force our fears on our daughters? Do we not make up symptoms, just like my mother made up symptoms of me going out of state for college? Do we not sometimes even cause symptoms by indoctrinating our daughters with debilitating fears?

Fear of any sort is a handicap that must be overcome. You're probably thinking, "I'm not projecting fear by teaching my daughter the dangers of the world." Let's not confuse fear with caution. To teach your daughter caution and vigilance is not the same as teaching fear. Telling your daughter how to avoid the potholes of life is different from telling her that she will ruin her life *because* of the potholes.

Even though my daughter also chose Tennessee State University for her post-secondary education, I still encourage her to do a lot of the things I was fearful of doing as a young adult, like travel and see the world and make some calculated, bold moves. I encourage her to take risks because I understand that growth and success are the biproducts of risk and failure. You cannot have the first without the latter. Will it hurt to see my daughter experience the heartaches, pains, bumps, and bruises of life's tests? Absolutely! But if I genuinely want the best for her, I must let her face them.

Therapy is Necessary

Therapy! Such a taboo word to some. But why? Why is seeking therapy so frowned upon in some cultures? I believe the reason is that we don't want to show that we are human. We don't want to admit our weaknesses. Yet, therapy exists to make us better humans, to equip us with more strength, and to get us on a clearer pathway forward.

Being in tune with her differing moods and attitudes, I sensed something was off with my daughter when she was around 17 years old. She has the brightest smile, but I could tell something was behind that smile, and it was not joy. I suspected that repressed feelings about my mom's passing seven years prior were the culprit. Sydnei had accomplished a lot in that timeframe, and she often remarked how she was sad that Ma Ma Ma was not here to witness it all. I assured her that Ma Ma Ma knew exactly what was going on and she'd been with her, with us, the whole time. She was still unhappy.

"What's wrong? Why do you seem so down?" I asked with a concerned look on my face.

"I don't know," she said quickly.

"Don't give me that. You have to know something," I said, getting a bit frustrated.

I continued on. "Okay. Let me put it this way. What is it that you don't have that you want or need?"

I thought I was doing a good job of being a present and supportive mother, so why was she getting a bit too aggressive in her speech with me, bordering on disrespect? She acted like she had a big chip on her shoulder, and it was really bothering me that I couldn't get anything out of her. I didn't like where we were heading as a mother/daughter duo at all.

After probing and prodding and asking tons of questions, she finally confided in me that she often felt overwhelmed, stressed, and unhappy. This came as a shock to me because, on the surface, she seemed the total opposite. She's a well-liked, popular girl who has a family that loves her and who supplies her every need. She was even crowned Prom Queen for goodness' sake! Wasn't that enough? No. Clearly not. She needed more—much more. She needed to do some internal work, the kind that I, as her mother, was not qualified to handle. I was extremely distraught by the notion that my child felt so hopeless. So, I put a call in to her pediatrician to get some advice. He suggested seeking out a life coach/therapist for help. I know several LCSWs so I reached out and got a referral to someone she trusted for us and eventually, she was hooked up with someone who could offer the help she needed. It was the best decision I've made so far because she is now equipped with an impartial, trained professional from whom she can get the necessary tools, coping skills and techniques to be healthy. Yes, she still sees this therapist even four years later.

In fact, we have both been to a counselor for myriad reasons—individually and collectively. In the current world we live in, anxiety and depression are at an all-time high. There are those who are qualified to help us tackle our "stinking thinking" or diminish the dark clouds above that seem to smother us and suck the life right out of us. Life requires us to refine and re-tune at different phases and it is our right to seek to always be the best we can be.

As her mother, I also have a responsibility to motivate, encourage, and uplift her when she feels overwhelmed—not to the degree of a qualified mental health professional, but as a confidante. I would remind her that the only way to eat an elephant is one bite at a time. Focus on what you can comfortably consume today and prepare the plan of attack for tomorrow. Do not borrow from today by worrying about tomorrow. Life evolves. It ebbs and flows. Your priorities, dreams, and drive at 21 won't be the same when you are 41. Let life happen naturally because things can easily shift, up or down, in the blink of an eye. If that's still not enough, professional help should be sought. Period. One of the most important principles I can teach my daughter is to take care of her whole self–mind, body, and spirit.

She has to fight for it. There are many attacks coming her way because she is destined for greatness! Therefore, I remind her that she has the power and the control to lift up and move those mountains out of her way, to keep her eyes on the prize and her goals in her heart. Life is not always going to go as planned, but in the end, everything will be fine. If not, it is not the end.

Mental health is a serious issue. Many times, we tend to overlook the emotions of our children. Mothers should be in tune with their children's moods and intervene when we see things are off track, because if it goes unchecked, it could have adverse effects on them or the people around them. In order to protect their fruit, it's paramount that we protect their emotional and psychological well-being.

Prepare the Soil

What will you do, now, to start speaking your daughter's love language?

_____
_____
_____
_____

What you speak and how you speak to your daughter becomes her inner voice. Why do you think this is important?

_____
_____
_____
_____

What is the difference in projecting fear compared to teaching caution?

_____
_____
_____
_____

Is seeking outside, professional help important to you? Why or why not?

_____
_____
_____
_____

Section 3
Preparing for the Seasons

The seasons of life inevitably turn, just like the seasons of nature. There are rainy spring days, hot and sweltering summer days, cool and refreshing fall days, and frigid winters. When the seasons change, we get a sense of where we are in life's cycle. Seasons are powerful! They have the force to change our moods and perspectives as Mother Nature intended. We also get a chance to evaluate our individual thoughts, beliefs, and value systems. As mothers and daughters, we must allow the seasons to transform us, enlighten us, and guide our emotional and physical resilience, as we prepare for the good times and the inevitable hardships that will come.

Winter

What thoughts come to mind when you think about winter? Is it an ending, a death or depression? Indeed, it's a dark season where nothing in nature blooms. The wintertime can feel pretty drab due to longer nights and shorter days. The beautiful green leaves are gone, and everything looks lifeless. However, the reason the trees are bare is because they have retracted all of the life-giving sap to their roots as a way to preserve themselves during the freezing and unfruitful winter.

Similarly, the winters of our lives are the same—cold, barren, and even painful. These are times when relationships are lost, death hits our families, or careers end. But, just like the trees, we must also retract our life-giving sap for introspection and self-examination. For the mother/daughter relationship, utilize the winter season to assess yourself, your feelings, behaviors, and attitudes.

Plot Twist!!

Negril, Jamaica, in the late fall of 2006: This was the backdrop to my ideal, island-infused wedding. After researching several local venues, caterers, and wedding planners, it seemed more economical, and more fun, to just go away and get married—a planned elopement, if you will. A destination package that included the wedding and honeymoon sounded too good to be true. The price was too! Literally, all we would have to do is show up and they would handle all of the details for a week's worth of celebrations. The all-inclusive resort had everything you can imagine—wonderful food, lively entertainment, and romantic beaches that looked like they were cut right out of a magazine. Our penthouse loft came with our own butler, who anticipated our every need: breakfast on the balcony, showing up with umbrella service when it rained, balancing cool towels on his head to give us as we basked in the sun that overlooked the Caribbean Sea. If this was any indication of how my marriage was going to be, then it was heaven-sent.

"PLOT TWIST!!!"

Fast-forward three years. It was an incredibly pretty, spring day—a Friday, so it was a dress down day. I got ready for work and put on some denim jeans, a pink AKA t-shirt, and pink sandals. I loved casual Fridays. I had a meeting scheduled with my supervisor at 9 AM so I arrived around 8:30 AM. It was a typical day. I normally

Preparing a Fruitful Harvest

called my mom every single morning at 9:30 AM to fill her in on all of the latest news and gossip from the night before. I was looking forward to our standing morning call.

When I got out of my meeting at around 9:20 AM, there was a group of co-workers surrounding my desk. My husband was also among them. It looked like one of my colleagues was shutting down my computer. I walked over with a confused look on my face.

"Hey y'all! What's up?"

They were all silent and just staring at me with a somber look. I turned to look at my husband whose eyes were bloodshot red as if he'd been crying.

"What's wrong?" I asked nonchalantly.

"Come with me," he said as he grabbed my hand and led me to the stairwell. "Get your purse," he added.

I pulled my arm back and said, "Where are we going? Why are we leaving? What has happened? Why are we going through the stairwell?" I questioned him relentlessly.

While we were in the stairwell, he turned around to me with tears in his eyes and mumbled, "Ma Ma Ma is at the hospital."

You see, this was the name that Sydnei gave her. When she was a baby and before she could talk, I would joke with her and say, "That's MY mama," obviously referring to my mother, her grandmother. She would retort and say "NO, MA MA MA." So, that's how my mother's name was born. She was affectionately known as Ma Ma Ma.

I gasped with my heart racing. "The hospital? Why?"

"Come on, let's go," he said as he pushed open the door that led out to the parking lot.

Before I walked out of the door, I screamed at the top of my lungs. "NOOOOOOO!!! What happened to Ma Ma Ma?"

He held me up by my waist and walked me to the car. I got into the car but didn't put my seat belt on. I was rebelling. I demanded to know what was going on.

My husband finally told me. "She's gone."

My mom had passed away hours earlier. Everyone knew but me. Everyone was just trying to figure out how to tell me. My confidante, my ride or die, my best friend was gone. My mom was my biggest cheerleader and supporter. She encouraged me and taught me the value of family. What she didn't teach me was how to live without her.

Christmas was her favorite season and she reveled in being able to bless others during the holidays. We also had our little quirky traditions where we would all gather at my grandparents' home to eat a big meal, sing Christmas carols, and pass out gifts. My mother was the songbird! She was a hard worker, a revered dance instructor, impacting the lives of preschoolers and senior citizens. She was beautiful!

She raised me to always think for myself and to go after my dreams. When I was a child, she was my role model. When I became an adult, she was my absolute best friend. We attended comedy shows together and made lasting memories going "down home" to Tuscaloosa, AL to visit our other relatives several times a year.

Who was I going to talk to now? We had hopes and dreams of starting a business together. She had fallen ill but wasn't really vocal with me about the details. I just knew that she was in and out of the hospital, for what she would call "some testing." I later learned that she just didn't want me to worry. She was actually at the end stages of congestive heart failure. All that time and I had no clue.

April 24, 2009 forever changed my life and my daughter's. My mom gained her heavenly wings, and a gaping hole was left in my heart. The biggest component of my village was gone.

Life was quite different afterwards. I was pretty sure I wasn't going to make it. However, about a year later, I learned that I was pregnant with a baby boy. WOW! This was a welcome surprise and surely a gift sent down from heaven to remind me that life goes on. Thanks, mama!

With all of the highs and lows, I was hit with yet another blow. My husband and I called it quits just two short years after our son was born. We filed for divorce. Not even that beautiful, heaven-sent wedding in Negril could keep us away from the devastating realities of divorce.

My young daughter was deeply immersed in all of these life events—the untimely passing of her grandmother and the breaking up of a blended family. It was, quite frankly, the best and worst season of my life. Simultaneously, I was grieving two losses. It was hard. I felt unloved, unwanted, lost, confused, and mentally drained on a daily basis, all while trying to raise a tween and a toddler. This was not the plan at all.

My daughter was watching. Through my pain, I had to turn these treacherous moments into teaching moments for her. I was always preaching to my daughter to take care of herself in mind, body, and spirit; to do things that make her happy and seek counseling to cope with the trials and tribulations of life. Now, I was on display, needing to take my own advice. So, I sought out counseling and developed a bucket list of items to make myself happy. Some of these were traveling, cutting my hair off, partying, and hosting girls' night out at my house. I was a single woman now and doing things that I wanted to do on my own time and my own terms. It was as if I got my groove back! But, I still had to come to terms with the fact that I was still in love with my ex-husband.

Eventually, life began to get back to normal and a few years later, my ex-husband and I found ourselves rekindling our relationship. He was still in love with me too! We both recognized that family was our main commitment and what we had set out to build together could still be a reality. We both grew up during our separation and were stronger for it. Our philosophy was that forgiveness, love, and hard work could bring us all back together where we belonged.

There was a difficult conversation that I needed to have with my daughter. There had been a level of dysfunction that she had seen for some time in the household, and she had formulated her own opinion about my ex-husband's character. I recently asked her what her real and raw thoughts were when I broached the conversation about us getting back together.

"I was mad and confused because I'm possessive over you. I was mad that he did all that and y'all got back together. But I was young and didn't know all the facts. When I got older, I didn't really care anymore. If it makes you happy, then it makes me happy," she confessed.

So, what would come of all this? Indeed, she had been a witness to the dysfunction that was playing out in our home. She had seen me go through the highs and the lows of being a divorcee—a real roller coaster ride. None of this was her fault or anyone's fault, really. My ex-husband and I both played a major role in the downfall of the marriage. I needed her to know that.

The overall teachable moment was that I, too, am human. I am capable of causing pain. People aren't going to always like me, and I have made and will make my fair share of mistakes. I am not immune to life's plot twists and turns—nobody is. I realized that being able to forgive and rebuild that trust was a virtue that my daughter should be shown. My ex-husband and I were interrupting the patterns of dysfunction and opening up dialogue about this very unpopular decision for us to come back together. "People can change, mama. I say, if you set someone free and they come back, it was meant to be." My daughter spoke those words to me as evidence that she finally got the lesson.

There is Purpose in Your Pain

Earlier this year, I attended a virtual panel discussion of mothers and daughters, hosted by a local church. I was also asked to moderate this particular conversation and was thrilled to accept the invitation. I had prepared several questions for the group, hoping to gain their take on: establishing and encouraging healthy mother/daughter relationships, seeking counseling, working towards individual and collective mental health, and surviving domestic and sexual violence. At times, the conversation was raw and real, especially the stories of trauma and abuse.

One mother and daughter provided a pre-recorded interview. The mother was my age with a daughter in her teens. I was provided the video days before, but I never looked at it. I had no clue what I was about to see and the impact it would have on me. Perhaps I wasn't ready to listen to a teenager talk about sexual abuse.

"And now, we have a video from young Maria and her mother, Mrs. Long," I said with excitement.

The video began with introductions. "Hello, my name is Ann, and I have survived sexual, emotional, psychological, drug and alcohol abuse."

"Hello, my name is Maria, her daughter, and I have survived sexual abuse."

I immediately felt a tugging at my heart as I was witnessing a generational cycle in real time.

Preparing a Fruitful Harvest

"Who was your abuser to you, Ann?" the voice of the interviewer chimed in.

"Family members, ex-boyfriends, and ex-husbands."

"And what about you, Maria?" The interviewer asked.

"He was my acquaintance. I wouldn't really consider him a friend, but if the event hadn't happened we probably would have been dating."

The interviewer asked about age.

"I was about 14 or 15," Maria confirmed.

"My abuse started around age 16 up until about a year or so ago," the mother stated.

Neither the mother nor the daughter told anyone about the abuse at first. I was curious to know why. Just then, the interviewer said, "What made you wait to tell someone?"

Mrs. Long explained that she kind of just dealt with it on her own, but she eventually told someone—someone who was like a second mother to her. The teen, Maria, didn't tell anyone at first because she blamed herself and said she just felt numb all over. She didn't realize she was even a victim of a sexual assault until the next day. Eventually, she confided in her school counselor. But the emotional damage was done. Her peers blamed her and unfortunately, Maria thought it was just what she deserved.

Her mother thought she was deserving of the abuse, too. As I watched the video in sheer amazement, I sensed a harrowing pattern that had been passed down from the mother to the daughter. At some point, the seeds of relational dysfunction were planted in both of them.

Luckily, both mom and daughter had support from each other and from other family members. Mrs. Long said she confided in her daughter. Imagine the burden on this teenager's shoulders, knowing the trauma her mom was experiencing. Later on, she fell victim to the abuse herself.

The interviewer asked, "What helped you get over it?"

"God," they said in unison. "God saved me from taking my life. I am here for a reason and that's to help my daughter and break generational curses. My daughter gives me strength. We are also in counseling now. It has changed our relationship, being there for each other, showing her how to be a stronger woman. I can talk to her, and she can talk to me. She's like my rock. It's helping me to see things from a different perspective."

"I've opened up a lot more," Maria said with a smile. "It's helped a lot."

The final question was asked of Maria. "What advice would you give other teenagers going through the same ordeal?"

"To hold on and to know that whatever it is, no matter what, it's not your fault. Get help even if you don't think you need it. In the long run, things will get better."

"WOW!!" I exclaimed after the video ended. "Thank you for trusting us with your vulnerability and your honesty, Ann and Maria! I am sure that was not easy to talk about, knowing it would be viewed by the public." Heads were nodding on my computer screen.

Preparing a Fruitful Harvest

"Let's talk about the state of your mind after that traumatic experience," I said concerningly. "Mental health is as important to our well-being as legs are to a table. What are some of the ways you take care of your mind and why is this important for you as a mother and a daughter?"

"I agree." Ann confirmed. "We must be willing to go to counseling, but also, we must tell our stories like we are doing right now on this panel. We can't be ashamed of what we've been through because I know it will help someone else."

Her daughter chimed in, "Yeah. It's been hard, but we go to counseling together and it's making me more confident to talk to girls all over so that they can see that they can overcome this."

"So, there's a purpose to your pain?" I asked, matter-of-factly.

"Absolutely!" the mother/daughter duo said in unison.

This panel of women warriors and tenacious teens taught me that there is always a purpose to our pain. Throughout the discussion, it was revealed just how resilient young girls are; and how mothers, despite the experiences they've gone through, can still prepare their daughters to be fearless, strong, unrelenting, and productive citizens of this world. That's generational health!

Spring

Spring is all about sowing new seeds. It's the planting season that symbolizes that life can begin again. Likewise, the springtime of our lives is full of fresh ideas and sowing the seeds of greatness in our daughters. It allows us to transition into a world of learning and opportunity. Life during springtime feels joyous, grateful, and energized. For the mother/daughter relationship, these days are to be cherished.

Utilize this time to identify your daughter's strengths and weaknesses and to teach her the principles of generational wealth, generational health, and generational blessings. Engage in refreshing conversations about solidifying future dreams and aspirations, taking special note of your well-being to get the most out of this rebirthing season.

The Fruits Of Your Labor

Have you ever heard of fruit astrology? It's a real thing. It reveals different personality traits behind your favorite fruits. The springtime is a good time to plant certain seeds. A simple Google search brought me to this website and as I thought about the different attributes of these fruits, I started to liken them to my daughter's temperament and strengths. As I dug deeper into this phenomenon, I was surprised at how accurate it was—for myself and for my daughter. On this journey to generational health, be sure to know what kind of fruit you want to plant. Let's examine some of that sweet, healthy, and delectable goodness.

Apple: She is a leader, outspoken, and extravagant.
Banana: She is soft-spoken, loving, and sympathetic.
Cherry: She is creative, kind, and loyal.
Orange: She is patient, hard-working, and reliable.
Peach: She is independent, friendly, and forgiving.
Pineapple: She is brave, honest, and an organized soul.

This is not an exhaustive list of fruits, so feel free to research on your own, but it definitely helped me to start speaking to the future in my daughter and finding ways to encourage her to come out of any comfort zones to realize her full potential. She was entering the middle school years when I realized that my daughter was a cocktail trio of apple, peach, and cherry: an independent, friendly, patient, hardworking, outspoken leader.

Guess what? Her fruit medley is different from mine. I am a mix of pineapple, apple, banana, and orange. Some people have even said that I have the patience of Job. It is really easy to want our girls to be and do the same things as we are and we do, and call them our little mini me's. For example, I began dancing at the age of three and so I enrolled her in dance classes at the same age. We completed one recital and called it quits. It just didn't stick. I quickly learned that she would rather join gymnastics, so we tried that out and just like a dismount, it stuck, and eventually afforded her the opportunity to be a cheerleader in middle school and high school.

Now, if I had pushed her to do dance when her passion was really toe touches and tumbling, she could have missed her opportunity to be the captain of the cheer squad her senior year. Our daughters are unique with their own likes and dislikes. I have learned and experienced great success when allowing my children to be their authentic selves, quirks and all. Otherwise, they would be miserable and not fulfill their innate purpose.

***

Leadership

Mamas!! We have the power to create the future leaders of tomorrow and to be the cheerleaders we so desperately needed when we were growing up. We especially have a duty to model the principles of visionary leadership to our young girls. We must teach them not to fit into glass slippers but to break glass ceilings, require them to be respectable, respectful, and respected, and lead them through the rough terrains of life. Show them that when they get knocked down, just yell **"PLOT TWIST!!!"** and keep it moving.

Lastly, let us share our cautionary tales, pitfalls, and mistakes so that we can help our daughters avoid them. We must remind them that real life happens while we are making other plans. And going through those temporary valley moments only ignites grit, gratitude, and grace–all of the components needed to live out loud with wisdom and vision, to make it to victory.

In March 1998, about eight months before I found out I was pregnant with my daughter, I chartered a graduate chapter of Alpha Kappa Alpha Sorority, Inc. in the city of Nashville, Tennessee. Throughout the years, I have held many different leadership positions within the sorority on the local, regional, and international levels.

I didn't want to always rely on grandparents and friends to babysit Sydnei while I was off doing my own thing, so I was determined to carry out my leadership duties as a single mother. To that end, she came along on this journey with me. If that meant taking her to meetings, conferences, banquets, community service projects, then so be it. She was going to witness me reaching my goals and going about my life pursuing my passion of serving others. When I became president of my chapter, she began to learn how to conduct business meetings.

One day she asked, "Mama, what does 'aye' mean?"

Preparing a Fruitful Harvest

"'Aye' means yes, baby," I replied.

"Why can't you just say yes?" she replied.

She could not understand why we couldn't just say "yes" or "no" when approving and rejecting a motion. That was her favorite part of the meetings and when we arrived back home, she would often imitate me presiding over the meetings, trying to use the terminology from Robert's Rules of Order.

When she turned 13 years old, I wanted to put her in environments that nourished her strengths and the leadership skills she had witnessed all those years. We decided to try Top Teens of America, Inc. Or maybe it was me that decided it for her. Let's be honest, she did not want to be a part. But I knew it would be good for her since she was coming of age and would be in college soon. I felt this organization would enhance her outspokenness, her loyalty, and her independent nature.

Top Teens of America, Inc. is a national teen organization that encourages high academic scholarship, developing social graces, and experiencing leadership. Among several thrusts, the teens are concerned for senior citizens, the uplifting of women, and the beautification of community. You have to be sponsored to be in this group, which means someone has to see something in you and invite you into the organization based on merit. Being a typical teenager, she was not impressed with having to get up early on Saturday mornings to attend meetings and outings. I assured her that this would be good for her in the long run. I was planting the seeds. During her tenure in

Top Teens, she was able to travel to different conferences all over the Southeast and meet other Top Teens from across the area. She learned the art of speaking, which was good, as she was quite bashful about talking in front of groups of people. She also developed leadership skills and forged lasting friendships with other like-minded teens from all across the country.

After about two years in this esteemed organization, that same little shy girl became the president of the local chapter. My daughter was asked to speak to the next incoming class of Top Teens. She told them how she was not thrilled to be in the organization at first. She talked about how fearful she was of public speaking. But now, she was encouraging her peers to come out of their shells and to show up for this once-in-a-lifetime opportunity. It was a full-circle moment for her that is still paying enormous dividends today. She has been the keynote speaker for various events around campus and in the community.

As moms, it is fulfilling to always look towards the future and the potential of our children. Even though my daughter dreaded being in this new space at first, she hadn't realized the leg up she was given. By enlisting her in this organization, I was positioning her to become the leader I knew she could be. I also wanted her to be surrounded by other goal-oriented teens who wanted more out of life than what was shown on TV or heard in the music of today. I wanted to prove to her that she *could* do it and do it well while still being a typical teenager. I nurtured these character seeds by being intentional about seeing the bigger picture for what she could do and be, as well as keeping the main thing the main thing—and that's knowing how to handle business. I was preparing her for adult life when bills and responsibilities come.

One of the proudest days of my life was when my daughter became my sorority sister in 2019. She entered into the sisterhood already ahead of the leadership curve because she witnessed it with me and now she is modeling it for future generations. Leadership is a powerful legacy for our girls. We are witnessing it right now with the historic inauguration of Senator Kamala Harris as the very first African-American and woman Vice President of the United States of America. Little girls everywhere can look up to her and know what's possible. Instead of being constantly told that they're *"bossy,"* they can be reminded that they are leaders in the making.

You, too, can recognize your child's character by placing them in different environments to see what piques their interest. When they are younger, pay close attention as they play make believe. What are they acting as? As they get older, talk with them about what they like or, as I like to call it, what makes them come alive. Is it music? Maybe working with their hands? Or do they like to talk? Really listen for the passion in their voice as they share their desires. Begin to look for opportunities to cultivate those character seeds by getting them involved in community organizations, school, or church activities.

The Fruitful Formula

Generational Wealth

Generational wealth is passed down from generation to generation in the form of leaving a legacy. That legacy could be money (wealth), heirlooms (sentimental jewelry), traditions (how we celebrate Christmas), values (honesty and hard work) and/or virtues (patience and faith). However, we will focus on the financial legacy. So, why should this be at the forefront of a mother's mind? Well, I am glad you asked. It's a seed that needs to be planted in our daughters to ensure that they have a leg and a hand up. Gaining financial wealth can provide more options to help them along the way. However, sometimes, there are roadblocks to leaving this kind of financial legacy. Having a warped sense of reality can cause us to think short term, only for today, and not worry about tomorrow, or the long term. We must change this mindset in order to pass down generational wealth.

Below are four fundamental steps I believe you will need to take to pass down generational wealth, from short-term to long-term goals.

Start a Savings and Investment Account

Starting a savings account is the easiest and your first priority in forging a path to generational wealth. It is quick to set one up with your bank. Try to save $1,000 in

90 days. If you think about it, that's just $11.11 per day. This is the goal that my financial coach gave me to work towards. However, you can decide what amount works for you. Just start somewhere! It can even be as little as a dollar a day. Make sure to also set up a savings account for your children, too. This could be in the form of a "save the change" savings account, CD's, or specific investment vehicles for a college fund. Other investment accounts such as IRA's and 401K plans for your retirement are also worth researching.

Become Financially Literate

Begin an in-depth study about finances and how money works. How can you teach what you don't know? There are many apps, books, and programs to learn how to handle finances. I took Dave Ramsey's *Financial Peace University* back in 2005, and it put me on a trajectory to learning so much about how money works. For an awfully long time, I thought money grew on trees. Unfortunately, having this mindset was a grave disservice when I grew up because I did not understand how to be a good steward of my money. Learning how to budget is a skill everyone needs to acquire as early as possible. Understanding the dynamics of saving vs. spending, investing vs. consumption, and assets vs. liabilities could make the difference between generational wealth or generational poverty.

There are downloadable spreadsheets that can help start you on your budgeting journey. It is also a good idea to learn the differences between good debt and bad debt. Credit cards are not always a bad thing! Learning how to use credit to build "good credit" is essential to creating wealth. Your financial literacy will have a major impact on your mother/daughter experience. It will impact the life you can provide your daughter today and how she manages money in the future.

Purchase Term Life Insurance

Now that you've started your savings and built your financial literacy, it's time to protect your daughter's future. You can do this by purchasing a term life insurance policy that will be passed down to your beneficiary in the event of your untimely death. It is extremely affordable, especially if you are young and in good health. A term life insurance policy is typically for a specific period of time, say 10, 20, or 30 years. A mother's death leaves an irreplaceable void of advice, counsel, and support. By providing financial inheritance, you can alleviate the burdens of your financial provision. Your insurance benefits can go towards future college tuition expenses for your children and/or other debt accrued. We know that everyone must pass on one day, so making plans to leave something to your children to be able to carry on with their lives financially is what generational wealth is all about.

Become a Homeowner

Lastly, home ownership is another leg up for our children. It has been widely reported that owning your home not only creates an asset for individuals to invest and acquire wealth, but it also helps build stable and strong families, thereby cultivating better communities. However, down payments and closing costs have hefty price tags and are often roadblocks. Having adequate savings can, oftentimes, take care of these requirements and alleviate a lot of stress and anxiety. Owning your home is a major step that may take some time and is a great long-term goal; however, you should make it one of your top priorities and examples in your pursuit of generational wealth.

Although these are the four steps I took to create generational wealth, I wanted to take it a step further. Specifically, when I became a mom, I wanted to make sure my daughter understood how the banking industry worked. I would take her with me to deposit and withdraw funds and explain to her how the money goes into this big, safe place. I could come and get money out anytime I needed. The value in exposing this to her early on was to instill a sense of responsibility and the virtue of patience; that money is an instrument that we control and tell what to do, not the other way around. It should be put aside for the things we need to take care of and for those things we enjoy. Today, she is fully aware of how easy it is to spend money, how disciplined you have to be to save money, and how rewarding it is to be able to be financially secure. With good financial acumen, jobs and other opportunities are out there for you. There's a sense of peace that provides a different outlook on life. That's what passing down generational wealth looks like.

My three steps to creating a generational wealth mindset are:

Change your mindset from lack to abundance to plenty, and from instant gratification to long-term success.

Teach your daughter about finances and reiterate how knowing how to be a good steward of her money can help secure her financial future.

Surround yourself and expose your daughter to a "village" of resources (i.e., people in the financial industries and those with knowledge of how to build wealth) who can help with any additional questions.

Generational Health

The definition of generational health is to ensure that the future generation is better equipped with the tools to be emotionally, mentally, physically, and financially sound than the previous generation.

When we look at our mothers, fathers, grandmothers, and grandfathers, we often see similar patterns in ourselves. That's just human nature. But are all of those patterns productive? If not, that's where we, as mothers, need to unlearn some of the things that we were taught growing up. For instance, you may have been taught that it is not acceptable to cry and that showing emotion is a sign of weakness. That's total BS! When I cry, I make sure not to hide it from my children. I also explain to them why I am crying so that they will know that crying is a form of cleansing and it can make you feel better, actually. You may have been told that mental health is just all in your head and going to therapy is useless. Maybe you were taught that getting physical and exercising your body is not important because, let's face it, we all will die anyway. When it comes to religion, you may have been indoctrinated into a certain faith because that's just how it was in your family.

Now that you're an adult, and more importantly, a mother, it is vital that you break any cycles that you believe are not for you and don't align with your ideals and life goals for you and your daughter. The goal is to instill in our daughters that with which we want our future grandchildren to be equipped.

Conversely, I can point to a particular generational health category that was positive for me in my upbringing and that has carried over to my daughter: the spiritual. My grandmother and mother left a legacy of faith within me, and I am now passing that legacy on to my daughter. I love that she got a tattoo on her shoulder of the Bible verse Romans 8:18: *"For I reckon that the sufferings of this present time are not worthy to be compared with the glory which shall be revealed in us."*

Generational health, for our daughters, is essential to their self-worth. How they feel about their upbringing and what they learned will carry over into every aspect of their lives. For instance, if there was a generational cycle of abuse and neglect in the home, statistics show that about 30% of abused and neglected children will later abuse and neglect their own children. These are the types of generational cycles we want to break, to present a different path for our daughters to follow.

My three steps to creating a generational health mindset are:

Be the change you want to see in your daughter. It starts with you, Mom! She is looking at your example of what healthy relationships should look like. If that means getting professional help for your past mistakes, then do it!

Know and understand your own self-worth so that you can cultivate self-worth in your daughter.

Declare that all negative generational cycles stop with you. When someone says, "It runs in the family," simply say, "It doesn't anymore!"

The Formula: Generational Wealth + Generational Health = Generational Blessings

You may be asking what all of this really means. Let me tell you a personal story. When I was a single mom, I still wanted the fairytale family: a husband, our daughter, and our dog. But that didn't happen. At least not with Sydnei's biological father. However, the void left in my daughter's life by her absent father was not easy to fill. I became unrelenting in my pursuit of the blessings that I knew were upon her life. I set out to teach her everything under the sun so that she would be fiercely independent in her finances, show integrity, and be a leader. I want her to know that she is worthy and should take care of her mental health. I want her to understand that mistakes are a part of the journey and to have faith that it will all work out for the greater good. Lastly, I want her to strive to do life a little bit better than I did.

I know that a lot of her abandonment issues stem from this void. She has asked me, "Why didn't he want me?" with tears in her eyes. Those types of questions broke my heart because I didn't have the answer. She's 21 now. There is nothing that she needs or wants, as I, along with my village, have provided extensively for her.

As a result, my daughter is fully aware of the intentions I've set for her: that what she experienced is not normal, that she deserves more, and that she does not need any sort of validation from anyone else to make a fruitful life of her own. She is much stronger and wiser. She is a hard worker who manages her finances well and is preparing to own her home in the next few years. She has gained clarity of who she is and what she wants out of this life. She doesn't want her future children to feel the way she was made to feel.

What I have learned through all of this is that the mother/daughter relationship is sacred ground. When there is a void, we must cancel the echoes of abandonment and mistrust in our children's lives and foster a mindset of value and worthiness. Just because a $50 bill is crumbled up, torn in half, or trampled on does not mean its value decreases. Even in those broken situations, it is still worth $50. I had to constantly remind my daughter of this throughout her adolescence. I am also a proponent of seeking the help of mental health professionals, if needed, to stop the cycle of dysfunction in our families, thereby allowing blessings upon us, our children, and our children's children. This is the generational blessing!

Summer

Summer is the nurturing season. It's a time for protecting our most precious assets. Summer expresses infinite growth potential because we are meticulous in our care and an abundance of light is available to us. This season is full of joviality! For the mother and daughter, summer is the time to bathe your daughters in the sunlight of your love, admonition, and encouragement. During this season, protect your daughter's growth by providing her with ways to support others and to find her passions.

Protect Your Fruit

Now that you have nurtured the seed of your fruit, how do you protect it? Being the leader that my daughter is and also a teenager in today's world of peer pressure and social media, I understood that I had to protect her fruit. We've all heard the phrase, "One bad apple can ruin the bunch." The Bible states it this way: "Evil communications corrupt good manners." (1 Corinthians 15:33). In other words, mothers cannot get comfortable and assume that because we see the growth of good fruit, that our jobs are done.

As mothers, we must be vigilant and guide our daughters to protect them from the forces that will ruin and tarnish their greatness. We must protect their eyes and their ears so that they will choose wisely. I took time to enter Sydnei's world of social media, music, and media to understand the slang, the idiosyncrasies, the gripping stratospheres of Instagram, Facebook, Twitter, SnapChat and TikTok. I did this so that I would be better equipped to speak her language and to open a lane of communication she could understand–meeting her where she is. In my opinion, there is no such thing as over-communication.

It is good to know who, what, when, where, why, and how in all cases. Those of us born in the 70's are not living in the same world in which our parents raised us. We have to be smarter, more vigilant and look to leave a lasting legacy for our children. Did you know that a girl's self

Preparing a Fruitful Harvest

-worth is improved when the women in her life cultivate and curate her uniqueness? With the rise of cyber bullying, body shaming and low self-image, we have a duty to combat all of those bad seeds by planting and harvesting the good seeds—mine being those of the apple, peach, and cherry. I challenge each of you to nurture the fruits of your labor.

Seek Your Passion

As our daughters get older, helping them find their passions in life is one of the most rewarding parts of the mother/daughter experience. It allows you to get inside of her head, to get a feeling of how her environment has shaped her sense of self. It is definitely a journey with winding roads and, sometimes, dead ends. I encourage you to have a sit-down and discuss the following prompts to help get the creative juices flowing. You never know, you may just find your passion as well.

I wanted to have a conversation with Sydnei as she was just a few months away from graduating from college. Gone are the days that we push working for a big corporation and fueling someone else's dream. Don't get me wrong, it is absolutely okay to travel that path. However, I wanted to cultivate an entrepreneurial mindset so that she could begin to find her passion and start evolving in it. I believe once we find our passion, we can create multiple streams of income.

"Syd, let's talk. Tell me how you would answer these questions I've prepared on seeking your passion."

She seemed a bit taken aback because that's what I do. Out of the blue and without warning, I ask questions. I also wanted to see if some of the seeds I've been planting were sticking as she enters adulthood.

"Ugh, Mama. Do we have to do this now?"

"Yes." I said sternly. "Step away from the phone for just a minute, honey. It'll be there."

"Question 1: What are your top three core values?"

"Loyalty, honesty, and family," she answered.

"Okay." I said. "Remember, your core values are your why in life. Why do you want to cultivate this kind of life and what do you expect from it? You will have to refer back to one or all of these often when you begin to craft your vision," I explained.

"Question 2: What do you want most in your life right now?"

She looked at me as though I should have known the answer.

"Money," she said. A typical response from a young adult, right?

I explained, "What you want most in life right now is your motivation to keep going."

"Question 3: What makes you smile and/or come alive?"

"Music makes me smile and traveling makes me come alive," she said.

"What makes you smile and/or come alive will keep you calm in the midst of struggles while on this journey," I explained.

"Question 4: Who do you admire?"

"I admire my mother," she responded.

"That's me!" I blushed.

"Question 5: Who inspires you?"
"I'm inspired by my mother."

I blushed again. I explained, "Who or what inspires you and who you admire will be your resources to glean wisdom and understanding about what you're going through, and to hold you accountable."

"Question 6: If money or time were not a factor, name one, big, crazy-faith goal?"

She paused and thought hard. "Ummm… I would visit each continent."

"Good one!" I commended her. "Your crazy-faith goal is just there for you to dream BIG and not limit your desires or capacity."

"Question 7: What is success to you?"

"Success is being paid to do what I love to do," she explained.

"Success looks different for everyone. That is why you have to define it for yourself and not worry about what is going on in another person's lane," I explained.

"Question 8: What one word describes you?"

"Outgoing." She answered that one quickly.

I explained, "How you describe yourself is how others will see you. It doesn't matter what anyone calls you. What you answer to reveals how you think of yourself."

This concluded the question-and-answer session. I was happy to see that she had a strong foundation to start crafting her passion in this life. Notice her answers to questions 4 and 5 above. This is why I am writing this book—to drive home the point that mothers change generations. If we plant the seeds, water the ground, give it light and love, we will enjoy a fruitful harvest.

Autumn P. Prather

Complete the activity below:

1. What are your top three core values?
___
___
___
___

2. What do you want most in your life, right now?
___
___
___
___

3. What makes you smile and/or come alive?
___
___
___
___

4. Who do you admire?
___
___
___
___

5. Who or what inspires you?
___
___
___
___

Preparing a Fruitful Harvest

6. If money or time were not a factor, name one, big, crazy-faith goal?

_____
_____
_____
_____
_____

7. What is success to you?

_____
_____
_____
_____

8. What one word describes you?

_____
_____
_____
_____

Fostering Friendships

Friendship is important because our daughters want to belong. We are all communal beings and thrive better in a tribe. I have always encouraged my daughter to develop meaningful friendships with those who share the same interests. One of my many highlights during Sydnei's teenage years was meeting and greeting all of her friends—guys and girls. Even though I often felt like my house was not *visitor-ready*, there would always be someone with her.

"Excuse this mess, sweetheart," I was always yelling through the house. But that didn't seem to matter. "You're fine, Ms. Autumn!" they would say, to ease my insecurities. They came right in and made themselves at home. That's exactly what I wanted.

Friendships are an important part of adolescence. Teenagers need to feel a sense of belonging and having close relationships with their peers helps them to have identity outside of their immediate families. I had a great time with my friends during my teenage years. Remember the Haunted Woods story I talked about earlier? We had a very tight posse, a group of girlfriends just hanging out together every chance we got. It was the best time of our lives.

Even though we were having fun, we were also developing compassion and empathy for one another. This is the core of teen friendships. But there's always another side, and I wanted my daughter to understand this. I have always told my daughter that it's important to find your tribe and nurture those friendships. It may take years to do this but it's worth it to have those connections. Connections are needed in this world of "it's not what you know, but who you know."

Whenever I engaged with Sydnei's friends, I reveled in the fact that they called me "Mama Autumn," or just simply "Mama," or "Mom Dukes." It really gave me a sense of peace knowing that her friends thought of me in that light. I was able to get to know all of them on a much deeper level. This was the goal. I wanted them to be able to trust me with anything, just like I wanted my daughter to trust me with anything too.

Isabel Allende said it best: *"I can promise you that women working together—linked, informed and educated—can bring peace and prosperity to this forsaken planet."*

Throughout my many years of service in the Sisterhood, I have come to understand the power of building community with other women. Indeed, a mother wants her daughter to be and feel supported by her close-knit group of girlfriends. Unfortunately, women get a bad rap when it comes to being in each other's corner. As mothers, we must break this cycle and nurture this skill within our daughters.

Below are my 5 S.T.E.P.S. These are five qualities all women should seek out and exude when fostering friendships.

S – Sisterhood – Sisterhood is the immeasurable power of women gathering together for a common purpose. Anything to the contrary is unacceptable. "Discord," "disrespect," and "demean" are words that should not be associated with your sister friends. Sisterhood is not a competition but a conduit to the meaningful, the magnificent, and the magical. There is no competition because when one of us wins, we all win.

T – Toughness – What's really admirable about women is their tenacity and tirelessness. Women are built with a toughness that is indestructible. Friendship requires toughness to weather the inevitable storms that will hit your relationship. As the R&B group New Edition sang, "Sunny days. Everybody loves them. Tell me baby, can you stand the rain?" Your friends must be tough enough to carry you when you are weak; handle the accountability that you must share in a true friendship; and protect you against those who seek to harm you—emotionally, physically, and mentally.

E – Empowerment – Women should lift each other up and propel each other forward in our pursuit of excellence. We should be comfortable enough to throw each other's names around in settings of great influence, and speak about our individual strengths in rooms of opportunities.

P – Purpose – Once women do the work to understand their God-given purpose, they become unstoppable. I tell my daughter all of the time that her circle of friends should challenge her to live out her purpose. They should

Preparing a Fruitful Harvest

push her to be the best she can be and pour into her as much as she pours into them.

S – Security – Being around friends should feel safe and should provide a safe place for your vulnerabilities. If you don't feel secure to share your passions or your pains, you will not have a healthy friendship.

The old adage states, "Show me your friends and I will show you your future." Mothers!! Help your daughters cultivate great friendships and show them how to be a great friend. No fruit grows alone. She needs the strength of a peer group to thrive. Help her to identify the 5 S.T.E.P.S. to her healthy friendships.

Fall

Fall (a.k.a. autumn) is the time of harvest! It's a culmination of our pain, our renewal, and our labor to protect and nurture our daughter's growth. It's a time to gather all we've learned through the previous seasons to reap a bountiful harvest. It's the season of life where we can get our last hoorahs in before the end of the year and take stock of all of the life lessons that have come our way. Autumn is a time of great change. The leaves are turning from a pristine green to a golden brown, which eventually fall down to the ground. The trees are now bare and lose their beauty, but only temporarily. It's a bittersweet season.

Fall demands that we go into preservation mode. For the mother/daughter relationship, this is a good time to let go of what no longer serves you and to stand on your mission to leave a lasting legacy, individually and collectively. It is also the time to reap your fruitful harvest.

Reap Your Fruitful Harvest

My pursuit of generational health is very intentional. Although becoming pregnant with Sydnei was a total shock and not in my plans, I knew I wanted to make her life as good as it could possibly be. But it would take me being a role model, a confidante, and eventually, a best friend.

When our daughters are little girls, we are their role model. No singer or rap artist or fashion model can replace our example and teaching. When they become teenagers, we are their confidantes. This is where communication and trust are most needed because life can get pretty topsy-turvy during these times. When they become adults, we become best friends because we've been developing that sacred bond since day one.

Without a doubt, my daughter is my best friend. She knows she can come to me for anything, and I know that I can confide in her. But, again, this was an intentional act and we both worked hard to get here. Believe it or not, we weren't always this close. There were times when I was at my wits end with the attitudes, the eye rolls, and all of the back talking. But over the years we have learned each other's love language and have found a common foundation on which to stand. Some of the things we have consistently done over the years that have gotten us to this point are:

Preparing a Fruitful Harvest

- Making daily phone calls to each other
- Family nights
- Spa days
- Doing yoga together
- Going to the mall
- Making TikTok videos
- Taking girls' trips
- Counseling each other

But it's especially important to understand that every flower that blooms had to go through a whole lot of dirt to get there. Think about that for just a moment. You have to know the quality of the soil in which you're planting. Is it healthy and fertile? You have to also make sure you have optimal exposure to sunlight and plenty of water in order for something to grow. Are you practicing self-care and leaning on your village for additional support? You must work this garden—ploughing, digging, and aerating for the best results. Are you looking for ways to enhance your daughter's skills and strengths?

However, there are times when a flower doesn't bloom or weeds take over, compromising its beauty. In this case, you must go back to the drawing board and assess the environment, not the flower. Are there still any generational cycles to break? Is there a need for therapy or counseling in your relationships? Sometimes you will still get wildflowers, and that's okay. It just means that they were strong enough to grow in the most unlikely of places, even in darkness, and rise up through the cracks and crevices of life.

Autumn P. Prather

Wasn't she just a preschooler? Wasn't I just braiding her long, curly hair into six ponytails, putting on her blue school dress, white tights, and Buster Brown shoes? I was just helping her to brush her teeth as she stood on a step-stool to reach the sink, and now she is a 21-year-old woman who is about to graduate from college and start her career. She is a leader in the community, at the university and within our sorority.

Was getting here easy? No. Do we still have a long way to go? Yes. In fact, "parenting" a 21-year-old is much harder because she's an adult now. I know I can't call all the shots anymore. She has to make her own decisions and mistakes. I have to allow that. It's scary! Letting her, and sometimes forcing her to be an adult is hard because we are used to being caregivers, fixers, and healers of the world.

As mothers, we want to do everything we can to shield and protect our daughters from heartache, pains of rejection, and health scares. Recently, we were faced with a particular health concern. She didn't feel that something was quite right with her body and she made an appointment with her doctor to get it checked out. It was a good thing that she did because it could have developed into a more serious health condition. I was so proud of her for taking care of and advocating for herself during this time. She showed real strength and wisdom. Like an adult!

Preparing a fruitful harvest is an ever-evolving journey. It requires patience, perseverance, faith, and fortitude. Just know that every seed will reap a harvest, no matter how long it takes. That's patience. Understand that you must continuously prune your daughter for healthy growth. That's perseverance. Allowing the different seasons to organically affect the mother/daughter relationship is faith. Hardships will come and life's cycles will test our resilience. Fortitude gives us peace in knowing that our strength to courageously raise our daughters, in a world that is constantly trying to tear them down, will surely bring about generational health.

Leave a Lasting Legacy

My senior year! The most exciting time of the year because graduation was near. Some of us were continuing on to college. Some were going into the military. Others were entering the workforce. Before we said our final farewells, the signing of the yearbooks was a highly anticipated event. The staff included a section in our yearbook where the seniors could bequeath something to the classes behind us. It was a really neat way for the upperclassmen to leave something to the "youngins."

"I, Autumn Everett, leave my majorette boots and my smile," I proudly wrote as my last will and testament. I was captain of the majorette squad and being one of the high steppers in the "Band of Distinction" was one of the highlights of my high school career. What I didn't realize was that there were many young girls who looked up to me and aspired to be one of the high steppers. I was somewhat of a role model. I carried my love of dance into my college days and became captain of the majorette team with Tennessee State University's "Aristocrat of Bands." Again, in college, I was inspiring hundreds of aspiring majorettes. I recently received a special note from someone who said she would break away from her family just to see me march into the stadium. Humbled!

Once I became a single mother, something clicked. I can't quite put my finger on it, but it was a spiritual awakening. Instinctively, I knew that my life would never be the same and that I would have to be overly cautious of everything I said and did, for there were little eyes watching my every move now. One of the biggest revelations was dating while being a single mother. There were many men who were coming in and out of my life. I had to make some hard decisions. Choices needed to be made. I was a mother now and had to make my daughter's needs a priority. She deserved stability. So, I had to be intentional about dating and the potential influence my chosen mate would have in my daughter's life. I had to be smart about this as well. I'd seen too many reality TV shows with women parading men in and out of their child's life, leaving behind confusion and blurred lines of what healthy relationships should look like. I was determined not to be that mama.

Contrary to what I thought my last will and testament was saying almost 30 years ago, I've learned over my years as a mommy that leaving a legacy is not at all about leaving something to a person; it is all about depositing a passion, a desire, a spark, and a quest for greatness in a person.

Before my mother left this earth, we talked about starting a business together. She was deeply passionate about senior citizens and housing, and she wanted to convert a building that she co-owned into a senior boarding house. I really wish that dream could have been realized for her.

In 2018, I had an elective surgery that, unfortunately, caused me to suffer a host of medical complications. During my recovery, I had an epiphany.

"If I hadn't gone back to the hospital a week after my initial surgery to see why I couldn't digest any food, I don't think I would have survived. That emergency, second surgery surely saved my life," I thought to myself.

Part of my bowel had literally died and had to be cut out. My recovery was going to be long and hard.

After I was released from the hospital, the day before Thanksgiving, I felt so incredibly lucky to be given a second chance, and I vowed that I would do something extraordinary with my life. As the saying goes, one day your life will flash before your eyes. Make sure it's worth watching. Mine sure did.

Then one day, it hit me. I remembered my mother wanted to start a business with me. She planted the seed of entrepreneurship and desired to create generational wealth within her family. Could this be a sign? Were Sydnei and I supposed to start our own business together to fulfill this prophecy?

My passion for empowering women, my love and devotion for my role as a mother, and wanting to honor my late mother in some way were the goals. I called a meeting with my daughter, who was still on winter break from college. She was already at home and I could lock her down. I took advantage of the moment.

"Ok! I got it!! We need to start a mother/daughter business," I said.

"Ohhh-kayyy," my daughter said hesitantly. "Is it a funeral home business?"

"NO!" I said, laughing.

Preparing a Fruitful Harvest

"Oh, okay. Let's do it!" she exclaimed.

"Okay. We need to work on a name, the purpose, the mission, and the vision." I said, "Oh, and we also need a tagline."

I had been researching how to start a nonprofit organization and found a suggestion that the shorter the tagline, the better. I also ran across information detailing each state's requirements of setting up this type of corporation. We have to choose a business name, check the database to make sure the name is not taken, file the formal paperwork, pay the appropriate fees, apply for tax exempt status with the IRS, and create bylaws.

Oh boy!!

What did I just get myself into?

I had nothing but time on my hands. I was recovering from two gruesome surgeries and to keep my mind occupied, I immersed myself in my new passion project.

On January 9, 2019, The Mother & Daughter Experience™ was born. Our chosen tagline, "Promoting Generational Health" was perfect! It encompassed everything we were about—a dynamic mother/daughter duo setting out to shine a light on the sacred, relational bonds of mothers and daughters so that these significant relationships are enhanced now and for generations to come.

To honor my mother, we created a memorial scholarship called The Mrs. Linda M. Everett ARTS Memorial Scholarship Fund, as she was an arts enthusiast. The goal is to offer scholarships to aspiring dancers. Our annual Mother/Daughter Breakfast is the biggest fundraiser to endow this fund and we cannot wait to give back to the arts community.

    Leaving a legacy is not about the tangible items we leave to our loved ones. I don't want to leave my daughter with things that can get lost, taken or stolen. I want to leave her with an awareness of her lineage and a longing to change the world in her own, unique way.

Flip The Script

Throughout my journey of spreading the word about our nonprofit, *The Mother & Daughter Experience*™, I have come across many women who did not have a good relationship with their mothers. I realized that everyone's experience was different. My mother and I had a great relationship and it was the reason I wanted to start the nonprofit.

I guess I was taking my relationship with my mom for granted. I honestly thought having a mutually respectful and thriving relationship was a fundamental fact of all mother/daughter experiences. Many of the stories I heard were heart-wrenching. There were mothers who just didn't care, mothers who were abusive and narcissistic, mothers who only knew how to survive and who were not emotionally attached to their children, and mothers who are not in contact with their daughters and therefore, do not have any contact with their grandchildren. Hearing this hurt my soul and I could see and sense the tears and trauma it brought up in those women recalling their stories.

One mom told the story of how it was her grandmother who cared for her and raised her. She called her grandmother "mom" because she said that's who nurtured her. I listened intently as she recounted how her grandmother was the one who instilled stability and strength into her, encouraged her to be the best she could be, and she credited her grandmother for leaving that legacy to her.

I really sat down with my thoughts surrounding the fact that it doesn't have to be your mother to leave a lasting legacy within you. It could be an aunt, a family friend, a special teacher, or anybody! A lot of the women I encountered were mothers of daughters. So, during a conversation on a popular social media app, I wanted to encourage them to turn it around. I stated:

"WOW! You are so strong. I see that not everyone grew up in a happy home or had the opportunity to experience healthy relationships as a little girl; so essentially, we have a lot of unhealed daughters navigating motherhood. However, you are still worthy of a flourishing lineage. You stood tall in your truth, but how can we remedy this lack of love, care and concern you experienced? You must flip the script and have that loving, lasting, relationship now with your daughter.

You know what it feels like as a daughter not to have that with your own mother. Don't allow your daughter to know that feeling too. Turn it around and deliberately right all the wrongs you faced. Leave the legacy you received from the positive role models in your life who instilled love, passion and honesty. If you didn't come from a healthy household, a healthy household must come from you."

Prepare for the Four Seasons

How have you experienced a purpose in your pain?
_____
_____
_____
_____

What "fruit" characteristics can you identify in your child that could shape her future?
_____
_____
_____
_____

How can you "protect your fruit?"
_____
_____
_____
_____

What legacy do you wish to leave to your child(ren)?
_____
_____
_____
_____